BREVET'S

ILLINOIS

HISTORICAL

MARKERS

and

SITES

Other Marker Titles:
- Nebraska Historical Markers & Sites
- North Dakota Historical Markers & Sites
- South Dakota Historical Markers & Sites
- Wisconsin Historical Markers & Sites

BREVET'S

ILLINOIS

HISTORICAL

MARKERS

and

SITES

Published by Brevet Press, Inc.

Copyright © 1976 by BREVET PRESS, INC.
a division of BREVET INTERNATIONAL, INC.
519 W. 10th St.
Sioux Falls, South Dakota 57104

Library of Congress Catalog Card Number: 75-253

Hard Cover Edition
ISBN: 0-88498-028-6

Soft Cover Edition
ISBN: 0-88498-029-4

First Printing 1976
Manufactured in the United States of America

TO
VANCE M. SNEVE

ACKNOWLEDGEMENTS

The editors wish to acknowledge each of several persons at the Illinois State Historical Library who gave extensively of their time and talents in the creation of this book.

First acknowledgement must go to Janice Petterchak, Curator of Prints and Photographs. Her research and assistance in obtaining the photographs and her knowledge of the historical markers program were invaluable to us in the preparation of this book.

Our special thanks to Al von Behren, staff photographer, in the preparation of the photos.

Thanks also to Lowell Anderson, Curator of Historic Sites.

We also wish to express our appreciation to William K. Alderfer, State Historian and Executive Director, Ozzie Reynolds, Historical Markers Supervisor, and all the staff of the Illinois Historical Society for their service in maintaining such an excellent historical markers program.

Our deepest thanks to all.

The Editors

Publisher: Donald P. Mackintosh
Editors: Lina S. Plucker-Kaye L. Roehrick
Consulting Editor: Tom Kakonis
Cover art and page art: Don Steinbeck
Initial Research: Vance M. Sneve
Printing: R.R. Donnelley, Chicago, Illinois

Composition and Layout: Enterprise Publishing Co., Inc.,
Flandreau, South Dakota

THE HISTORICAL MARKERS PROGRAM

Forty years ago, in 1934, the Illinois State Historical Society initiated a markers program to commemorate historic sites within the state. Since 1934 nearly three hundred markers describing persons, events, or areas important to the history of the state have been erected. Each marker is cosponsored by at least one local organization.

The majority of the markers are made of cast aluminum and are approximately three by four feet in size. Each marker contains a descriptive text of approximately sixty-five words in yellow lettering on a dark-blue background. The seal of the state of Illinois is engraved at the top of the marker, and the name of the local cosponsor is included in the credit line following the text.

In 1962, four-by-eight-foot plywood markers were introduced by the Society to detail broader aspects of state history. Those markers are cosponsored by the Illinois Department of Transportation. Each plywood panel, mounted in a rustic wooden frame, contains approximately 250 words of text in white lettering on a blue background. A white silhouetted map of Illinois is in the upper right corner of the marker. Decisions about subjects for both aluminum and plywood markers are made by the Historic Sites Advisory Committee of the Illinois State Historical Society; the Department of Transportation specifies the location for each of the plywood markers. The plywood markers are of three types: (1) entrance markers, titled "Thy Wondrous Story, Illinois," which narrate portions of Illinois history and are erected along major routes leading into the state; (2) area markers, usually located at highway rest areas or other park-like settings, which describe nearby historic sites; (3) city markers, erected along major routes, which give short histories of the cities and surrounding areas.

The markers program is administered by the historical markers supervisor, who is responsible for authenticating the historical facts for each marker subject, writing the marker inscriptions, and directing arrangements for dedication ceremonies. The final decisions concerning the acceptability of a site and the wording for each marker are made by the Historic Sites Advisory Committee.

Janice Petterchak
Curator of Prints
Curator of Prints & Photographs

Reprinted from the Journal of the Illinois State Historical Society, June, 1974.

CONTENTS

Southern Illinois

The Plains

Northern Illinois

MARKER KEY

Illinois has a variety of marker styles. To assist the reader in locating and identifying the markers, the historical legend has been enclosed in a stylized marker design similar to the actual marker.

MAP KEY

To assist the reader, the state of Illinois has been divided into three geograpic parts. This book follows the geographical divisions - each with its own color key. The color-keyed maps indicate the position of the marker or historical site in the state.

RED
Southern Illinois

BLUE
Northern Illinois

GREEN
The Plains

SOUTHERN ILLINOIS

Retiry Defences   Terminus of Cairo and Fulton RR.   Bird's Point.

CAIRO AND ITS VICINITY, ILLINOIS, LOOKING SOUTH, FROM THE ST. CHARLES HOTEL.—FROM A SKETCH BY OUR SPECIAL ARTIST.

Cairo and its vicinity, looking south from the St. Charles Hotel.

Located: (1) East side US 51, 1.5 miles north of junction US 51 and Illinois 3. (2) US 60-62 near entrance to Fort Defiance State Park.

OFFICIAL STATE MAP: P-6
ALEXANDER COUNTY

CAIRO, ILLINOIS

Pierre Francois Xavier de Charlevoix, a French Jesuit, reported as early as 1721 that the land at the confluence of the Mississippi and Ohio Rivers would be a strategic location for settlement and fortification. Nearly a century later, in 1818, the Illinois Territorial Legislature incorporated the city and bank of Cairo. But Cairo was then only a paper city, and plans for its development came to a standstill with the death of John Gleaves Comegys, the leading promoter of the corporation.

The area's commercial potential again captured the imagination of Illinois leaders and eastern investors in the 1830's. New city promoters incorporated the Cairo City and Canal Company and made elaborate plans for levees, canals, factories and warehouses. The first levees failed to hold back the rampaging rivers, and financial difficulties slowed the commercial boom. Company policy to lease, not sell, city lots also retarded expansion. With the first sale of lots in 1853 and the completion of the Illinois Central Railroad from Chicago to Cairo late in 1854, the city began to prosper.

When the Civil War began, both northern and southern strategists recognized the military importance of Cairo. On April 22, 1861, ten days after the bombardment of Fort Sumter, troops arrived to hold Cairo for the Union. They established camps on the land south of Cairo, and the city flourished as a troop and supply center for General Ulysses S. Grant's army. Although the city bustled with wartime activity, non-military commerce was reoriented along east-west lines.

STEAMBOATS ON THE MISSISSIPPI RIVER

In 1817 the **Zebulon M. Pike** reached the St. Louis, the farthest north a steamboat had ascended the Mississippi River. The western steamboat of later years was a credit to the frontier American mechanic who drew upon experience to build a large craft (eventually over 300 by 40 feet) which would carry heavy cargoes in shallow water against the strong Mississippi current. Owners boasted that steamboats could run on a heavy dew but in fact seasonal variations in river depth limited their use--medium sized steamboats needed at least four feet of water. The influence of the steamboat spread far and wide in the Mississippi Valley--sometimes farther and wider than expected when a boiler exploded--and hastened the development of the region.

Snags, explosions, collisions and fires sank many steamboats. An 1867 investigation recorded 133 sunken hulks in the Mississippi between Cairo and St. Louis, a stretch rivermen called the "Graveyard."

Even as the north-south river trade flourished in the 1850's transportation lines running east and west developed. Railroads which followed a more direct route than winding rivers and defied the seasons began to haul freight to and from the Mississippi Valley. Steamboats aided the North in the Civil War, but the reorientation of civilian commerce foreshadowed their decline. Although they continued to churn the Mississippi for the rest of the nineteenth century, even on the river, barges guided by a single steamboat or later by a diesel boat transported the cargoes which individual steamboats had carried.

Located: Illinois 3 near Thebes.

Steamboats on the Mississippi.
Illinois State Historical Library

OFFICIAL STATE MAP: O-6
ALEXANDER COUNTY

Located: South side of Illinois 146, 1500 feet east of the Mississippi River bridge near McClure.

OFFICIAL STATE MAP: O-6
ALEXANDER COUNTY

THY WONDROUS STORY, ILLINOIS

The fertile prairies in Illinois attracted the attention of French trader Louis Jolliet and Father Jacques Marquette as they explored the Mississippi and Illinois Rivers in 1673. France claimed this region until 1763 when she surrendered it to Great Britain by the Treaty of Paris. During the American Revolution George Rogers Clark and his small army scored a bloodless victory when they captured Kaskaskia for the Commonwealth of Virginia, and Illinois became a county of Virginia. This area was ceded to the United States in 1784, and became in turn a part of the Northwest Territory and the Indiana and Illinois territories. On December 3, 1818, Illinois entered the Union as the twenty-first state.

Many of the early settlers came from Kentucky, Tennessee, and the southeastern coastal states to live in the southern quarter of Illinois. As the better land was taken up, the line of settlement advanced northward. Within the southern portion of the state, Kaskaskia on the Mississippi River was the territorial and the first state capital, and Vandalia was the second state capital.

Northeast of this point, in Jonesboro, Abraham Lincoln debated with Stephen A. Douglas during the 1858 senatorial campaign. When Civil War broke out in 1861 troops rushed from Chicago to Cairo at the southern tip of Illinois to control the Mississippi River traffic.

Early pioneers coming to Illinois found that a lot of hard work awaited them in clearing the land for settlement.

Illinois State Historical Library

4

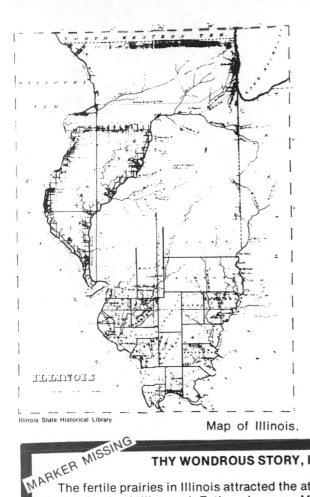

Illinois State Historical Library

Map of Illinois.

OFFICIAL STATE MAP P-6
ALEXANDER COUNTY

Located: US 60-62 near entrance to Fort Defiance State Park.

THY WONDROUS STORY, ILLINOIS

SEE HISTORIC ILLINOIS

The fertile prairies in Illinois attracted the attention of French trader Louis Jolliet and Father Jacques Marquette as they explored the Mississippi and Illinois Rivers in 1673. France claimed this region until 1763 when she surrendered it to Great Britain by the Treaty of Paris. During the American Revolution George Rogers Clark and his small army scored a bloodless victory when they captured Kaskaskia for the Commonwealth of Virginia, and Illinois became a county of Virginia. This area was ceded to the United States in 1784, and became in turn a part of the Northwest Territory and the Indiana and Illinois territories. On December 3, 1818, Illinois entered the Union as the twenty-first state.

Many of the early settlers came from Kentucky, Tennessee, and the southeastern coastal states to live in the southern quarter of Illinois. As the better land was taken up, the line of settlement advanced northward. Within the southern portion of the state, Kaskaskia on the Mississippi River was the territorial and the first state capital, and Vandalia was the second state capital.

The Third Principal Meridian, which U.S. 51 roughly parallels, was a basic line in surveying the Northwest Territory to establish definite land claims. The highway passes near Jonesboro where Abraham Lincoln and Stephen A. Douglas debated in 1858, and through Vandalia where Lincoln was a state legislator and cities in central Illinois where he practiced law.

5

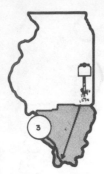

OFFICIAL STATE MAP: P-6
ALEXANDER COUNTY

Located: Ill. 3, in Lansden Park. West side of Walnut St. near intersection with Charles St. in Cairo.

Illinois State Historical Library

General Ulysses S. Grant, from an engraving by J. R. Rice.

THE **TIGRESS** FLAGPOLE

The river packet **Tigress** commandeered by the Union Army, carried General U. S. Grant up the Tennessee River to the Battle of Shiloh on April 6, 1862. A year later the **Tigress** was sunk while running the shore batteries at Vicksburg, Mississippi. The crew survived and returned her flagpole to Cairo.

West Side of Main Street of Palestine, Illinois.

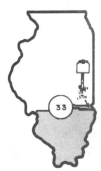

Located: Ill 33 in Palestine.
Main and Grand Prairie Sts.

OFFICIAL STATE MAP: J-10
CRAWFORD COUNTY

AUNTIE GOGIN'S STORE

On this block Mary Ann (Elwell) Gogin operated a general merchandise store in the late nineteenth century. One of the first women in Illinois to own and manage her own store, Mrs. Gogin was affectionately known as "Auntie" to the residents of Palestine.

7

CULLOM HOMESTEAD

Here stood the home of Edward N. Cullom who with Joseph Kitchell platted the village of Palestine in 1818. They donated to the county the land including the public square for the county seat. Early court sessions were held in the Cullom home.

OFFICIAL STATE MAP: J-10
CRAWFORD COUNTY

Located: Ill. 33, 208 S. Jackston St., Palestine.

Courthouse and Land Office.

OFFICIAL STATE MAP: J-10
CRAWFORD COUNTY

Located: Ill. 33 309 S.
Lincoln, Palestine.

Illinois State Historical Library

Jesse K. Dubois, owner of the Dubois Tavern, was a close friend of Abraham Lincoln.

DUBOIS TAVERN

Here stood the Dubois Tavern. Jesse K. Dubois, a close friend of Abraham Lincoln, was an official in the United States Land Office in Palestine from 1841-1842 and from 1849-1853 and later became Auditor of Public Accounts for Illinois. His son, Fred T. Dubois, became a Senator from Idaho.

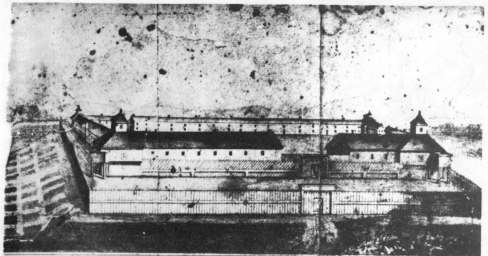

Early fortifications were built to protect soldiers and settlers from hostiles. Note the garden on the left, used to feed inhabitants.

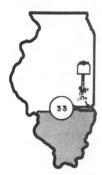

OFFICIAL STATE MAP: J-10
CRAWFORD COUNTY

Located: III. 33 west of Palestine.

FORT FOOT

About 1813 the William Eaton family and other restless pioneers considered Fort LaMotte too crowded and therefore constructed a new stockade on a site several hundred yards north of here. A family trait of the Eatons, large feet, led to the name Fort Foot.

FORT LAMOTTE

About 1812 the settlers in this area built Fort LaMotte for protection from hostile Indians. The pioneers farmed the adjoining land but stayed within easy reach of the protective walls. After the War of 1812 the Indian threat diminished and the inhabitants of the fort became the nucleus of Palestine.

OFFICIAL STATE MAP: J-10
CRAWFORD COUNTY

Located: Ill. 33 in Palestine, east section.

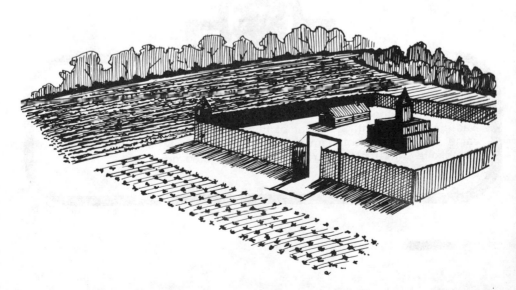

11

Illinois State Historical Library

OFFICIAL STATE MAP: J-10
CRAWFORD COUNTY

Located: U.S. 33, South
Pike and Grand Prairie Sts.,
Palestine.

Augustus French was the ninth governor of
Illinois.

GOVERNOR AUGUSTUS C. FRENCH

On this site stood the home of Augustus C. French (1808-1864) when he
was elected the ninth governor of Illinois. The early settlers in Illinois
came mostly from southern states so that French, a native of New
Hampshire, was the first "Yankee" to be elected governor.

Main street, Palestine, Illinois.

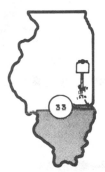

OFFICIAL STATE MAP: J-10
CRAWFORD COUNTY

Located: Grand Prairie and
Lincoln Sts., Palestine.

HOUSTON-DICKSON STORE

Two early residents of Palestine, John Houston and Francis Dickson, purchased this lot as the site for a combination dwelling and store about 1818. By 1820 their stock of merchandise provided nearby settlers with goods which they previously had to bring from Indiana.

13

Reality on the Plains, from Harper's Weekly, July 29, 1876, shows the heavy toll taken on both sides during Indian skirmishes.

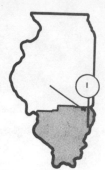

Located: Ill. 1 in Hutsonville, Illinois.

HUTSON MEMORIAL

Hutsonville was named after the Isaac Hutson family massacred by Indians in 1813 at a spot sixty-four rods due east of this marker. Hutson was killed later in a skirmish with the Indians near Fort Harrison, Indiana.

KITCHELL GRIST MILL

In this area Joseph Kitchell who settled here in 1817 erected a grist mill and distillery which eliminated the trip to Shakertown, Indiana where the farmers had previously taken their grain. Horses were used for power, grain was taken in pay, converted to whiskey and sold to the settlers.

Located: On Ill. 33 at south edge of Palestine.

Fort LaMotte as it appeared in 1811.

Locations: (1) North side of Illinois 33 at the northwest edge of Palestine in turnout with "Fort Foot" small marker. (2) West side of Illinois 33. 7 miles south of Palestine.

OFFICIAL STATE MAP   J-10
CRAWFORD COUNTY

PALESTINE, ILLINOIS

This area reminded Frenchman John LaMotte of the land of milk and honey, Palestine. While a member of the LaSalle exploring party, he became separated from the group, traveled down the Wabash River, and first gazed upon the region in 1678. Other French settlers came during the 18th century. Then, by 1812, the westward moving Americans began constructing Fort LaMotte. As the palisade filled with settlers, those desiring more room moved a few miles to the northwest and established Fort Foot.

The settlers in Fort LaMotte were the core of the town of Palestine. Platted in 1818 by Joseph Kitchell and Edward Cullom, the settlement served until 1843 as the Crawford county seat. The growth of the town lagged until a United States Land Office, opened in 1821, gave new importance to the community. Then, people came to buy land, to attend court, for entertainment, and to have their grain milled. Others, like Abraham Lincoln in 1830, passed through the bustling town on their way to settle in Illinois.

The land office continued to give prominence to Palestine. Robert A. Kinzie came in 1831 to purchase 102 acres for $127.68, an area which became the nucleus of Chicago. Augustus C. French (1808-1864) served as a receiver in the land office from 1839 to 1843. A native of New Hampshire, he was the first "Yankee" to be elected governor of Illinois. Chosen in 1846, French was forced to stand for re-election under the new constitution of 1848 and won.

UNITED STATES LAND OFFICE

A United States Land Office was located at this site in 1820 and operated until 1855. Settlers from as far as Chicago came here to file on homesteads. Young Abraham Lincoln, passing through Palestine in 1830 with his family in emigrant wagons, noticed a crowd before this land office.

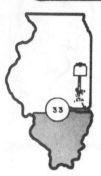

Located: Palestine, Illinois
on Illinois 33 .

OFFICIAL STATE MAP: J-10
CRAWFORD COUNTY

Settlers came from as far as Chicago to file on homesteads at the United States Land Office. This pioneer log cabin is typical of those the homesteaders built. Illinois State Historical Library, taken from John Drury's MIDWEST HERITAGE

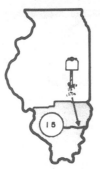

Illinois State Historical Library

Location: Ill. 15, west of Albion

William Pickering.

ABRAHAM LINCOLN

Spoke in the oak grove of General William Pickering north of here in the presidential campaign of 1840.

He was stumping southern Illinois as a Whig elector for General William Henry Harrison in the Tippecanoe and Tyler Too campaign.

In 1861 Lincoln appointed Pickering governor of Washington Territory.

THE ILLINOIS CENTRAL RAILROAD

On September 27, 1856, near this site, workmen drove the spike which completed the 705 miles of the Illinois Central Railroad's charter lines and the first federal land grant railroad in the United States.

In 1850 Congress had granted the alternate sections of public land within six miles on either side of the railroad between specific sites to the State of Illinois. The following year the state issued a charter to the Illinois Central which outlined the route from the southern end of the Illinois and Michigan Canal (LaSalle) to Cairo with branches to Chicago and, through Galena, to the banks of the Mississippi River. As construction advanced the Illinois Central received about 2,595,000 acres.

The Illinois Central developed the surrounding territory to assure an increasing business. They conducted an intensive publicity campaign by sending pamphlets and agents to the eastern states, Canada, England, Germany, Norway and Sweden to encourage immigration to Illinois. The company sold its fertile prairie land on liberal credit terms and settlers moved to the previously undeveloped region along the Centralia Chicago branch. In later years, the Illinois Central encouraged the development of a variety of crops such as sorghum, sugar beets, cotton, fruits, vegetables and soybeans; the improvement of livestock; the use of farm machinery; and the development of industry and coal mining.

For sixteen years the Illinois Central was exclusively an Illinois railroad; then it began to expand into other states.

OFFICIAL STATE MAP: K-8
EFFINGHAM COUNTY

Location: Northeast edge of Mason on Illinois 37.

"Locomotive Number 1," first of the Illinois Central's fleet, Circa 1863.

Illinois Central Gulf Railroad Corporate Relations Department

Illinois State Historical Library

Col. Robert Blackwell.

Located: US 40 & 51
Southeast corner of 3rd and
Gallatin Sts., Vandalia.

BLACKWELL'S WHITE HOUSF

Colonel Robert Blackwell's new two-story frame store and boardinghouse opened on this site in time for the convening of the Ninth General Assembly on December 1, 1834. He advertised board and lodging for "thirty or forty."

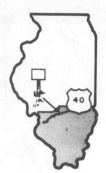

OFFICIAL STATE MAP: K-7
FAYETTE COUNTY

Located: Northwest corner of 4th and Gallatin Sts., Vandalia.

CHARTERS HOTEL

John Charters operated a large tavern on this site from the late 1820's to November 1835. Under the name, "Sign of the Green Tree", it was operated by Thomas Redmond until 1838.

Charters Tavern, Vandalia.
Illinois State Historical Society

CUMBERLAND ROAD

Vandalia was the western terminus of the Cumberland or National Road which extended eighty feet wide for 591 miles from Cumberland, Maryland through Pennsylvania, Ohio, Indiana.

Illinois construction by the Federal Government began in 1811 and ceased in 1838, the approximate cost being seven million dollars.

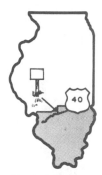

OFFICIAL STATE MAP: K-7
FAYETTE COUNTY

Illinois State Historical Library

The "Maddona of the Trail" statue marks the western terminus of the Cumberland Road at Vandalia.

FIRST STATE CAPITOL
1820-1823

The first Capitol building owned by the State was erected on this site. It was a thirty by forty feet two-story frame structure. The Second and Third Illinois General Assemblies met here, the House on the first floor and the Senate on the second. This building was destroyed by fire on December 9, 1823.

Located: Fifth Street in Vandalia.

OFFICIAL STATE MAP: K-7
FAYETTE COUNTY

21

Flack's Hotel in Vandalia.

OFFICIAL STATE MAP K-7
FAYETTE COUNTY

Located: US 40 Southeast corner Fourth and Gallatin Sts., Vandalia.

FLACK'S HOTEL

In 1836 Colonel Abner Flack took over the large three-story frame building which stood here, and operated it under the name Vandalia Inn. In 1853-1854 it was the headquarters for Chief Engineer Charles F. Jones, in charge of construction of the Illinois Central Railroad.

HISTORIC VANDALIA

Vandalia was the second capital of Illinois, 1820-1839. Here met the General Assembly, the Supreme Court, the Federal courts. Abraham Lincoln served in the House of Representatives 1834-1839, and Stephen A. Douglas 1836-1837.

The sites listed below have been marked.

1. Third State Capitol
2. Ernst Hotel
3. House of Divine Worship
4. Robert K. McLaughlin Home
5. Ebenezer Capps Store
6. Second State Capitol
7. Charters Hotel
8. First State Capitol
9. Public Printer
10. Flack's Hotel
11. Second State Bank
12. Vandalia Inn
13. Blackwell's White House
14. Cumberland Road
15. Old State Cemetery

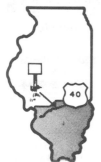

OFFICIAL STATE MAP: K-7
FAYETTE COUNTY

Illinois State Historical Library

Located: Vandalia State-house (State Memorial).

State Capitol, Vandalia.

Located: Main Street, Vandalia.

OFFICIAL STATE MAP: K-7
FAYETTE COUNTY

HOUSE OF DIVINE WORSHIP
Erected in 1823

The Illinois General Assembly donated five lots in Vandalia to promote the construction of a church for the use of all denominations. The forty-five by sixty feet one-story frame structure erected in the summer of 1823 was used primarily by the Presbyterians and Methodists and also for public meetings and as a schoolhouse.

OLD STATE CEMETERY

The Illinois General Assembly authorized Governor Edward Coles in 1823 to convey to Vandalia one and one-half acres for a state burial ground. Here were buried four members of the legislature and several state officials who died while in office. The monument erected by the state is in adjoining South Hill Cemetery.

Edward Coles, governor of Illinois from 1822 to 1826.

Illinois State Historical Library

Located: Edwards third, Vandalia.

OFFICIAL STATE MAP: K-7
FAYETTE COUNTY

OFFICIAL STATE MAP: K-7
FAYETTE COUNTY

Located: Old US 40, east of
the Kaskaskia River, east of
Vandalia.

Albert Gallatin

THE NATIONAL ROAD IN ILLINOIS

The National Road was the result of the project of Albert Gallatin to unite the East and West. His plan to allocate money from public land sales for this purpose was incorporated into the Ohio Enabling Act in 1802. The original road, as proposed in 1805 and authorized by Thomas Jefferson in 1806, was to extend from the Potomac to the Ohio. Construction began in 1811 and by 1818 the road was completed to Wheeling, Virginia. Two years later Congress agreed to extend the road and allocated funds for a survey through Ohio, Indiana, and Illinois.

The route from the Indiana line to Vandalia, approximately 89 miles long, was surveyed in 1827. In 1830 Congress appropriated $40,000 for opening and grading the Illinois section. Additional money was granted each year thereafter, but was limited to clearing, grading, and bridging. Construction problems and corrupt practices resulted in the project's being placed under the Army Corps of Engineers in 1834. The road was opened to Vandalia in 1839; however, the Illinois section remained an unfinished surface with only 31 miles of grading and masonry completed.

The road had been surveyed to Jefferson City, Missouri, but in 1840 Congress terminated construction at Vandalia. On May 9, 1856, Congress transferred the "rights and privileges" connected with the road in Illinois to the state. It became a part of the "National Old Trails Road" in the early twentieth century and was, until recently, a part of US 40.

PUBLIC PRINTER

This is the site of a two-story frame building occupied by Robert Blackwell, state printer 1818-1832, and publisher of the laws of the United States. In 1823 he became the publisher of the **Illinois Intelligencer** newspaper. The first periodical in Illinois, the **Illinois Monthly Magazine**, was printed here in 1826. Colonel Blackwell (1792-1866) was a member of the Illinois House of Representatives 1832-1836 and Senate 1838-1840.

OFFICIAL STATE MAP: K-7
FAYETTE COUNTY

Located: Gallatin Street, Vandalia.

Illinois State Historical Library

The Blackwell Printery in Vandalia.

ROBERT K. MCLAUGHLIN HOME

On this site lived Robert K. McLaughlin, state treasurer 1820-1823, state senator 1828-1832, 1836-1837, and register of the Unites States Land Office 1837-1845. Here the governors of Illinois resided when the Legislature was in session. The McLaughlin home was the social center during the time the capital was in Vandalia.

Located: Main near Third, Vandalia.

OFFICIAL STATE MAP: K-7
FAYETTE COUNTY

SECOND STATE BANK
1836-1865

The second State Bank in Vandalia was chartered in 1835. In 1836 an imposing two-story brick building with stone front and a porch with massive pillars was erected. It burned on March 4, 1865.

OFFICIAL STATE MAP: K-7
FAYETTE COUNTY

Located: Gallatin Street, Vandalia.

SECOND STATE CAPITOL
1824-1836

The second Capitol owned by the state was a two-story brick building erected here in 1824, using the walls of the first state bank which burned January 28, 1823. Abraham Lincoln was a member of the House in the 1834-1835 and 1835-1836 sessions. Vandalia paid one-fifth of the total cost of $15,000. Torn down in 1836, the salvage was used in the third Capitol building.

Location: Fourth Street, Vandalia.

27

Vandalia in the 1800's. The Capitol is visible at the far right.

SITE OF EBENEZER CAPPS STORE

During the years when Vandalia was the state capital (1820-1839), here stood the Ebenezer Capps Store, the largest wholesale and retail establishment in southern Illinois.

Located: Northeast corner of 4th and Main Sts., Vandalia.

OFFICIAL STATE MAP: K-7
FAYETTE COUNTY

SITE OF ERNST HOTEL

Here stood a two-story log building erected in 1819 for Ferdinand Ernst who brought the German colony to Vandalia. Named Union Hall, it was operated as a hotel. After Ernst's death in 1823 it was managed by E. M. Townsend, and from April 1825 by Frederick Hollman.

OFFICIAL STATE MAP K-7
FAYETTE COUNTY

Located: Southeast corner of Third and Main Sts., Vandalia.

THIRD STATE CAPITOL
Erected in 1836

The third Capitol building owned by the state was restored as a memorial in 1933. It was the Capitol from December 3, 1836 to July 4, 1839. Abraham Lincoln was a member of the House during the three sessions of the legislature held in this building, and was the leader in the removal of the capital to Springfield. Stephen A. Douglas was a member of the 1836-1837 session. The Fayette County Courthouse occupied this building 1839-1933.

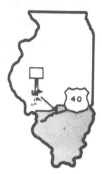

OFFICIAL STATE MAP: K-7
FAYETTE COUNTY

Located: Vandalia State House State Memorial.

Illinois State Historical Library

This mural shows the Third State Capitol in early Vandalia.

VANDALIA INN

The "very large tavern house, called the Vandalia Inn" opened here on November 15, 1834 with thirteen lodging rooms and a large dining room. Some years later it was known as Matthew Thompson's Tavern and was depot for the Overland Stage. It was destroyed by fire in June 1853.

Located: Third and Gallatin Sts., Vandalia.

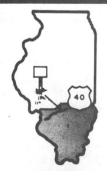

OFFICIAL STATE MAP: K-7
FAYETTE COUNTY

Vandalia became the state capital one year after Illinois gained statehood. The date of this early photo of Vandalia is uncertain.

Located: Visitors' Center. Rt. 51. Vandalia.

OFFICIAL STATE MAP: K-7
FAYETTE COUNTY

VANDALIA, ILLINOIS

For twenty years this city on the west bank of the Kaskaskia River was the capital of Illinois. In 1819, a year after Illinois gained statehood, the General Assembly voted to move state offices to Vandalia from Kaskaskia. The Second General Assembly convened at Vandalia, December 4, 1820, in the first state-owned Capitol. A second statehouse was used from 1824 to 1836. A third, built by Vandalia citizens in 1836 in an attempt to retain the seat of government at Vandalia, is still standing. Ownership of the building was accepted by the state in February, 1837, only a few weeks before the Assembly voted to relocate in Springfield, nearer the center of the state.

Officers of the first six administrations served in Vandalia. Here in 1836 Abraham Lincoln was admitted to the Bar of Illinois. Here also he began his political career in 1834 as a member of the General Assembly. Other prominent Illinoisans at Vandalia included legislators Stephen A. Douglas and James Shields, and James Hall, state treasurer, 1827-1831, and editor of **Illinois Monthly Magazine**, the first literary magazine in the state. The Illinois artist James W. Berry made his home here.

Vandalia was the terminus of the National Road, which began in Cumberland, Maryland. Authorized during Thomas Jefferson's administration, the National Road was the first highway built with federal funds. Vandalia is today the principal city and county seat of Fayette County. The restored third Capitol is owned and maintained by the state of Illinois.

Located: 204 South Main,
Benton.

Illinois State Historical Library

John A. Logan who is credited with formally
establishing Memorial Day in 1868.

JOHN A. LOGAN HOME

John A. Logan, Civil War major general, resided on this site, 1856-1861.
Logan was an U.S. Representative, 1859-1862, 1867-1871; U.S. Senator,
1871-1877, 1879-1886; and candidate for U.S. vice president in 1884. As
commander of the G.A.R.; his general order no. 11, May 30, 1868, formally
established Memorial Day.

This photograph of an oil painting of the Sears mill and dam near Rock Island is representative of the early mills of Illinois.

OFFICIAL STATE MAP: M-9
GALLATIN COUNTY

Located: Ill 141, Town hall, New Haven.

BOONE'S MILL

Jonathan Boone, brother of the famous pathfinder Daniel Boone, built a mill on this site about 1800. He was born in Pennsylvania in 1730 and died here about 1808. His son Joseph continued to operate the mill. In 1813 Joseph was named to mark out a road from Burnt Prairie to Shawneetown by way of his mill. On August 24, 1814, he purchased the millsite from the Federal Land Office at Shawneetown. The mill was used as a landmark by the State Legislature in describing the boundary line separating White from Gallatin County. Joseph sold the land in February 1818. He died in Mississippi in 1827.

Illinois State Historical Library

Civil War Major General Michael K Lawler.

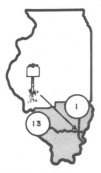

OFFICIAL STATE MAP: N-8
GALLATIN COUNTY

Located: Ill. 1 & 13, east of Equality

GENERAL MICHAEL K. LAWLER

Born in Ireland in 1814, Michael K. Lawler came here to Gallatin County in 1819. After serving as a captain in the Mexican War, he lived on his farm near here until the outbreak of the Civil War. In May 1861 he recruited the 18th Illinois Volunteer Infantry regiment, of which he became colonel. Lawler was wounded during the siege of Fort Donelson. In November 1862 he was commissioned brigadier general, and he fought gallantly in the campaign of Vicksburg in 1863. He became a major general in 1865, returning home the next year. He died in 1882.

JAMES HARRISON WILSON

James H. Wilson, American Army officer, engineer, and author, was born in 1837 on his family's farm about a mile south of here. He attended Shawneetown schools, McKendree College, and the United States Military Academy. In the spring of 1864, during the Civil War, he commanded Sheridan's Third Cavalry Division. In the spring of 1865, as brevet major general chief of cavalry, Military Division of the Mississippi, Wilson led a month-long mounted campaign through Alabama, capping his exploits by surmounting the fortifications at Selma. Detachments under his command captured Jefferson Davis. Wilson also served in the Spanish-American War and the Boxer Rebellion. He died in 1925.

James Harrison Wilson commanded Sheridan's Third Cavalry Division during the Civil War. Detachments under his command captured Jefferson Davis.

Illinois State Historical Library

Located: Shawneetown mall, Shawneetown.

OFFICIAL STATE MAP: N-9
GALLATIN COUNTY

Located: Illinois 142 south of Illinois 13 near Equality.

OFFICIAL STATE MAP: N-8
GALLATIN COUNTY

OLD SALT WORKS

One mile south was located one of the oldest salt works west of the Alleghenies. Here Indians and French made salt, while at a later day Americans established a commercial salt industry which finally attained a production of 500 bushels a day. The industry was abandoned in 1875.

The salt well in Gallatin County.

RAWLINGS' HOTEL

One of Shawneetown's earliest brick buildings, Rawlings' Hotel, stood on this lot. It was built in 1821-1822 for Moses Rawlings, who owned it until 1841. On May 7, 1825, it was the site of a reception held for the Marquis de LaFayette during his visit to America, 1824-1825. Accompanied by Illinois' Governor Edward Coles and other dignitaries, Lafayette walked between two long lines of people from the river's edge to the hotel. The building was one of eleven destroyed by fire, June 23, 1904.

OFFICIAL STATE MAP: N-9
GALLATIN COUNTY

Located: Ill. 13, Ohio River levee. Old Shawneetown.

Illinois State Historical Library

The Rawlings Hotel was the site of a reception held for the Marquis de Lafayette during his visit to America in 1824-1825.

OFFICIAL STATE MAP: N-9
GALLATIN COUNTY

Illinois State Historical Library

Shawneetown flood.

Located: North side of Illinois 13 about 2 miles west of the Ohio River bridge at Old Shawneetown.

SHAWNEETOWN, ILLINOIS

Ancient mounds rise above the low ground of Gallatin County in several places to testify to a prehistoric life and the northern section of Shawneetown rests on burial mounds. By the middle of the 18th century the Shawnee Indians had established a village here.

The first settler arrived about 1800 and others soon followed. The Federal Government laid out Shawneetown in 1810, before the surrounding area was surveyed. The town grew as the trading post and shipping point for salt from the United States Salines near Equality and as a major point of entry for emigrants from the east. In 1814 the United States Land Office for Southeastern Illinois opened at Shawneetown.

Two state memorials, the first bank in territory (1816) and the imposing state bank building (1839), in old Shawneetown mark the community's early prominence as the financial center of Illinois. According to legend several Chicagoans applied for a loan in 1830 to improve their village but were turned away because Chicago was too far from Shawneetown to ever amount to anything.

The Ohio River which contributed to the early importance of the town was always a threat to its existence. In 1937 the angry yellow waters rushed over the levees and rose in the town until they lapped the second floor of the State Bank building. It was then that most of the residents moved northwest to the hills and rebuilt Shawneetown, although some still clung to the original site.

Ferry on the Ohio River.

OFFICIAL STATE MAP N-9
GALLATIN COUNTY

Located: North side of Illinois 13, about 2 miles west of the Ohio River Bridge.

THY WONDROUS STORY, ILLINOIS

The fertile prairies in Illinois attracted the attention of French trader Louis Jolliet and Father Jacques Marquette as they explored the Mississippi and Illinois Rivers in 1673. France claimed this region until 1763 when she surrendered it to Great Britain by the Treaty of Paris. During the American Revolution George Rogers Clark and his small army scored a bloodless victory when they captured Kaskaskia for the Commonwealth of Virginia, and Illinois became a county of Virginia. This area was ceded to the United States in 1784, and became in turn a part of the Northwest Territory and the Indiana and Illinois territories. On December 3, 1818, Illinois entered the Union as the twenty-first state.

Many of the early settlers came from Kentucky, Tennessee and the southeastern coastal states to live in the southern quarter of Illinois. As the better land was taken up, the line of settlement advanced northward. Within the southern portion of the state, Kaskaskia on the Mississippi River was the territorial and the first state capital, and Vandalia was the second state capital.

This highway passes through an area rich in the early history of Illinois. It crosses the Ohio River where ferry service began about 1802, skirts old Shawneetown which was a major gateway for immigrants to Illinois and passes near Equality where the United States Salines produced salt for the Midwest in the nineteenth century. In 1937 a devastating flood covered most of Gallatin County and Highway 13 was under about ten feet of water.

This mural depicting a salt mining operation is in Gallatin County Courthouse.

Located: West side of Illinois 1. 2.4 miles south of the junction of Illinois 1 and 13 near Equality.

OFFICIAL STATE MAP: N-8
GALLATIN COUNTY

THE UNITED STATES SALINES [EQUALITY]

Two salt springs in Gallatin County produced brine for one of the earliest salt works west of the Alleghenies. One spring is just southwest of Equality and the other is a short distance west of this site. The Indians made salt here long before the first settlers appeared. In 1803 the Indians ceded their "great salt spring" to the United States by treaty. Congress refused to sell the salt lands in the public domain but it did authorize the Secretary of the Treasury to lease them to individuals at a royalty. The leases required the holder to produce a certain quantity of salt each year or pay a penalty.

Although the Northwest Ordinance prohibited slavery in this area, special territorial laws and constitutional provisions permitted exceptions at these salines. The lessees brought in Negroes as slaves or indentured servants and used them extensively in manufacturing salt. The census of 1820 for Gallatin County listed 239 slaves or servants.

In 1818. as part of the process of making a new state, Congress gave the salines to Illinois but forbade the sale of the land. The state continued to lease the springs and used the revenue to finance part of its operating expenses. Eventually Congress allowed the outright sale of the land. The commercial production of salt continued here until about 1873 when the low price for salt made the expense of extracting it from the brine prohibitive.

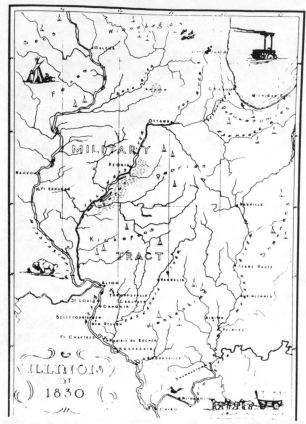

Located: "Scenic View," Ill. 149, Sand Ridge Township, east of Grimsby.

Illinois State Historical Library

Brownsville, southeast of Kaskaskia, is shown on this 1830 map of Illinois.

CONRAD WILL OF BROWNSVILLE

Dr. Will, the "Father of Jackson County," was born in Pennsylvania in 1779 and came to Illinois in 1813. He was a physician, but also operated a grist mill, tannery, and salt works in this area. He was one of the founders of Jackson County and in 1816 donated land for Brownsville, the first county seat. Dr. Will was a delegate from Jackson County to the First Illinois Constitutional Convention. He served in the General Assembly from 1818 until his death in 1835. When Will County, Illinois, was created in 1836, it was named in his honor.

FIRST COAL MINE

The first coal mining operations in Illinois took place in the Big Muddy River bluffs one quarter mile west of here. These outcroppings not only supplied local needs, but at an early date--perhaps as early as 1810--coal from them was sent by flatboat to New Orleans.

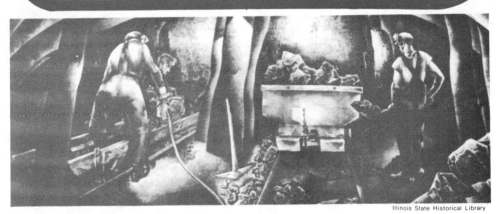

Illinois State Historical Library

Coal mining in Illinois, from a mural by William Schwartz.

Located: On north side of State Rt. 127 at east end of bridge over Big Muddy River east of Murphysboro.

OFFICIAL STATE MAP: N-6
JACKSON COUNTY

Location: "Scenic View" Ill. 149, Sand Ridge Twp., east of Grimsby.

OFFICIAL STATE MAP: N-6
JACKSON COUNTY

KASKASKIA RESERVATION

For a number of years prior to 1833, a few Kaskaskia Indians, remnants of the once-powerful Illinois, lived on a small reservation two miles south of here. The Indians ceded their lands to the United States in 1832, and relinquished possession the following year.

APPELLATE COURTHOUSE

This building was constructed for the southern division of the Illinois Supreme Court, one of three divisions created by the Constitution of 1848. Court met in lodge halls in Mount Vernon prior to completion of the center section of this building about 1857. The 1870 constitution established a system of appellate courts and Mount Vernon was named the seat of the Fourth District. The Supreme Court shared the building until 1897, after which all of its sessions were held in Springfield.

Located: Interstate 57 & US 460 at the Court house grounds, Mount Vernon.

OFFICIAL STATE MAP: L-7
JEFFERSON COUNTY

Illinois State Historical Library

Located: U.S. 460, S.E. of Mount Vernon.

Appellate Courthouse in Mount Vernon.

GOSHEN ROAD

The Goshen Road was one of the main arteries of travel in the early 1800's, when Illinois was frontier country. The road ran in a northwesterly direction from Shawneetown to Edwardsville--a distance of more than 150 miles. Shawneetown and Edwardsville were two of the leading commercial towns in Illinois. In the vast area between these towns most of the early settlements were along the Goshen Road, which was three miles east of this point in Jefferson County. In 1821, after the county was organized, an alternate road was surveyed in order to pass through Mt. Venon, the county seat.

LINCOLN IN LAWRENCEVILLE

In 1840 Abraham Lincoln, as a Whig elector, campaigned in southern Illinois for William Henry Harrison, Whig presidential candidate. Here in Lawrenceville, on October 28, he had a dispute with a local physician, William G. Anderson, who the previous August had run as a Democrat and lost the election for state representative. In writing to Lincoln on October 30, Dr. Anderson said that Lincoln was the "aggressor" in the dispute and that his "words imported insult." Lincoln denied the charge, saying that he regretted the incident.

Badges

Located: U.S. 50 Court-house, Lawrenceville.

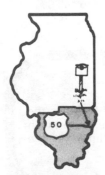

OFFICIAL STATE MAP: K-10
LAWRENCE COUNTY

43

Illinois State Historical Library

The Lincoln Trail monument in Lawrenceville.

Located: US 50 at Vin-
cennes bridge.

OFFICIAL STATE MAP: K-10
LAWRENCE COUNTY

LINCOLN NATIONAL MEMORIAL HIGHWAY

From the Wabash River to the Sangamon five miles west of Decatur, the
Lincoln National Memorial Highway follows substantially the route taken
by the Lincoln family in their migration from Indiana to Illinois in the
spring of 1830.

THY WONDROUS STORY, ILLINOIS

The fertile prairies in Illinois attracted the attention of French trader Louis Jolliet and Father Jacques Marquette as they explored the Mississippi and Illinois Rivers in 1673. France claimed this region until 1763 when she surrendered it to Great Britain by the Treaty of Paris. During the American Revolution George Rogers Clark and his small army scored a bloodless victory when they captured Kaskaskia for the Commonwealth of of Virginia, and Illinois became a county of Virginia. This area was ceded to the United Stated in 1784, and became in turn a part of the Northwest Territory and the Indiana and Illinois territories. On December 3, 1818, Illinois entered the Union as the twenty-first state.

On Dubois Hill nearby, an advanced prehistoric Indian group, the Riverton Culture, had a settlement from 1500 to 1000 B.C. They lived in semi-permanent settlements here and at two other known sites ten and twenty miles to the north on the Wabash River. They stayed in the settlements during bad weather and stored crops which they had raised here.

Toussaint Dubois settled on the hill about 1807. He was a well-known fur trader in partnership with Pierre Menard, first Illinois lieutenant governor, and owned some 4500 acres of land including the site of Lawrenceville. His son, Jesse K. Dubois, was a prominent office holder and was state auditor from 1857 to 1864. Jesse K. was a close personal friend of Abraham Lincoln from 1834 until Lincoln's death. Lincoln campaigned in this area in 1856 upon his invitation.

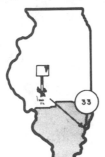

OFFICIAL STATE MAP K-10
LAWRENCE COUNTY

Located: West side of Illinois 33. 3½ miles northwest of the Ohio River Bridge near Vincennes, Indiana.

Cylindrical pit, Riverton Culture site.

by Winters. Howard Dalton The Riverton Culture, 1969.

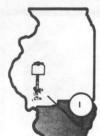

OFFICIAL STATE MAP K-10
LAWRENCE COUNTY

Location: At the foot of Main Street, near the ferry landing and at the entrance to the City Park, in St. Francisville.

TO VICTORY, FEBRUARY 25, 1779

On February 5, 1779, Colonel George Rogers Clark and his army began the difficult march from Kaskaskia to Fort Sackville at Vincennes. At daybreak on February 21 they began to cross the swollen Wabash near here. They went on to capture Fort Sackville and thus establish a firm American foothold in the northwest.

Illinois Sesquicentennial painting of George Rogers Clark.

Illinois State Historical Library

Location: U.S. 50 Red Hills State Park.

OFFICIAL STATE MAP: K-10
LAWRENCE COUNTY

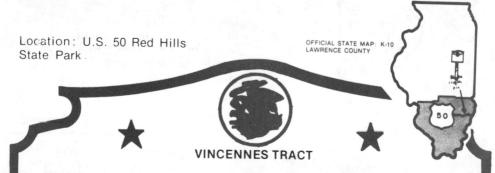

VINCENNES TRACT

The western boundary of the Vnicennes Tract passed through this point. The line extended south-southwest thirty-nine miles from present-day Crawford through Lawrence, Wabash, and Edwards counties in Illinois. The Vincennes Tract was seventy-two miles wide. About six-sevenths of it lay in Indiana. The Illinois portion was the first parcel of land in the Illinois country ceded by Indians. The land was ceded in the Treaty of Greenville, August 5, 1795, and confirmed in a treaty at Fort Wayne, June 7, 1803. Acting for the United States, William Henry Harrison, governor of Indiana Territory, negotiated the 1803 Treaty with the Delaware, Shawnee, Potawatomi, Miami, Eel River, Wea, Kickapoo, Piankashaw, and Kaskaskia tribes. Illinois was then a part of Indiana Territory.

FIRST STATE PRISON IN ILLINOIS

Ruins of first state prison in Illinois. Built in 1830-31. Unsanitary conditions aroused persistent criticism from Dorothea Dix, pioneer in prison reform. All inmates were transferred to Joliet prior to 1860. During the Civil War many Confederate prisoners were incarcerated here and deaths averaged six to ten a day.

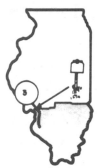

OFFICIAL STATE MAP K-4
MADISON COUNTY

Located: Broadway and Williams Streets, Alton

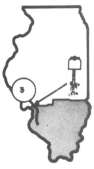

OFFICIAL STATE MAP: K-5
MADISON COUNTY

Located: On west side of State Rt. 112 one and ½ miles northwest of Edwardsville

Illinois State Historical Library

Dorothea Dix

MARKER MISSING

FORT RUSSELL

One-quarter mile to the west stood Fort Russell, a wooden stockade which served as a base of supplies and operations for the Illinois militia during the War of 1812. From here, for months at a time, Governor Ninian Edwards administered the affairs of Illinois Territory.

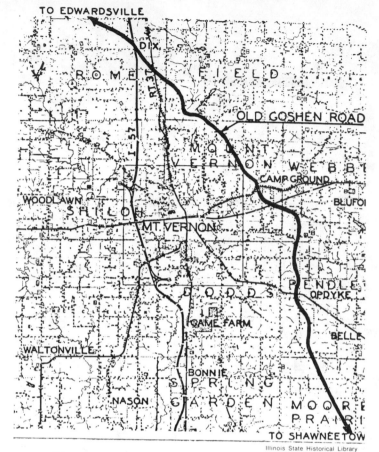

Illinois State Historical Library

This map shows the Old Goshen Road between Shawneetown and Edwardsville.

Located: Lewis & Clark Library, Edwardsville

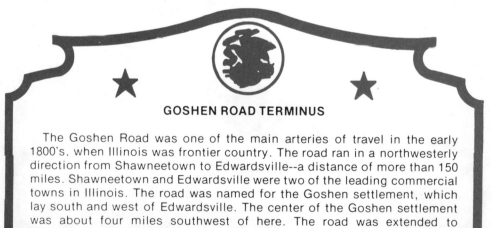

GOSHEN ROAD TERMINUS

The Goshen Road was one of the main arteries of travel in the early 1800's, when Illinois was frontier country. The road ran in a northwesterly direction from Shawneetown to Edwardsville--a distance of more than 150 miles. Shawneetown and Edwardsville were two of the leading commercial towns in Illinois. The road was named for the Goshen settlement, which lay south and west of Edwardsville. The center of the Goshen settlement was about four miles southwest of here. The road was extended to Edwardsville by 1814 and Alton by 1839.

Governor Edward Coles. who was convicted in 1824 of illegally freeing his slaves.

OFFICIAL STATE MAP: K-5
MADISON COUNTY

Located: At site of court-house in 1824. Edwardsville. Edwardsville High School grounds on US 66.

GOVERNOR COLES AND SLAVERY

Site of the courthouse where in 1824 political enemies convicted Governor Edward Coles of illegally freeing his slaves.

"To preserve to a continuous line of generations that liberty obtained by the valor of our forefathers. we must make provisions for the moral and intellectual improvement of those who are to follow."

LEWIS AND CLARK EXPEDITION

Meriwether Lewis and William Clark originally planned to camp west of the Mississippi River during the winter of 1803-4. Carlos Dehault Delassus, the Spanish commandant at St. Louis, however, had not received formal notification from his government of the Louisiana Purchase and would not permit the expedition to cross the river. Thus in the middle of December, 1803, Clark led about twenty-five men to the winter camp on the American side at the mouth of the Wood River, then 1¼ miles southwest of this site.

At Camp River Dubois Lewis and Clark gathered supplies, compiled information and trained their men. Originally there were nine Kentuckians, fourteen soldiers, two French watermen, one hunter-interpreter and Clark's Negro servant at the camp. They were energetic, healthy individualists who did not accept discipline willingly. During the winter Lewis reprimanded several men for refusing to obey the orders of other officers, failing to perform sentry duty and making "hunting or other business a pretext to cover their design of visiting a neighbouring whiskey shop...."

Additional recruits enlisted for the first part of the trip through hostile Indian country and in the spring three boats loaded with provisions, ammunition and merchandise were prepared for the long journey from the Mississippi to the Pacific Ocean and back. On May 14, 1804, Clark and about forty-five men "Set out at 4 oClock P.M. in the presence of many of the neighbouring inhabitents, and proceeded on under a jentle brease up the Missourie...."

Located: West side Illinois 3 (formally US 67 Alt) about 900 feet north of Ferguson Avenue in Wood River.

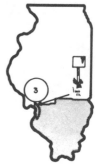

OFFICIAL STATE MAP K-4
MADISON COUNTY

William Clark and Meriweather Lewis.
State Historical Society of North Dakota

This early painting shows the mouth of the Missouri River which threatened early explorers.

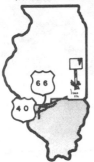

OFFICIAL STATE MAP K-4
MADISON COUNTY

Located: Bypass US 66-40 between Chain-of-Rocks Bridge and Illinois 3.

THY WONDROUS STORY, ILLINOIS

The fertile prairies in Illinois attracted the attention of French trader Louis Jolliet and Father Jacques Marquette as they explored the Mississippi and Illinois Rivers in 1673. France claimed this region until 1763 when she surrendered it to Great Britain by the Treaty of Paris. During the American Revolution George Rogers Clark and his small army scored a bloodless victory when they captured Kaskaskia for the Commonwealth of Virginia, and Illinois became a county of Virginia. This area was ceded to the United States in 1784, and became in turn a part of the Northwest Territory and the Indiana and Illinois territories. On December 3, 1818, Illinois entered the Union as the twenty-first state.

The Missouri River mouth, now 3½ miles north of this site, threatened the first explorers. The account of the 1673 expedition reported that while "sailing quietly in clear and calm Water we heard the noise of a rapid, into which we were about to run. I have seen nothing more dreadful. An accumulation of large and entire trees, branches, and floating islands, was issuing from the mouth of The river pekistanoui (Missouri), with such impetousity that we could not without great danger risk passing through it. So great was the agitation that the water was very muddy, and could not become clear."

During the winter of 1803-4 Meriwether Lewis and William Clark camped with their men at the mouth of the Wood River, at that time opposite the mouth of the Missouri, before beginning their famous journey.

OFFICIAL STATE MAP: K-4
MADISON COUNTY

Located: East side of US
67, 1.6 miles north of the
junction of Illinois 267 and
US 67 near Alton.

Daguerreotype of James Shields who challenged
Abraham Lincoln to a duel in 1842.

MARKER MISSING

THY WONDROUS STORY, ILLINOIS

The fertile prairies in Illinois attracted the attention of French trader Louis Jolliet and Father Jacques Marquette as they explored the Mississippi and Illinois Rivers in 1673. France claimed this region until 1763 when she surrendered it to Great Britain by the Treaty of Paris. During the American Revolution George Rogers Clark and his small army scored a bloodless victory when they captured Kaskaskia for the Commonwealth of Virginia, and Illinois became a county of Virginia. This area was ceded to the United States in 1784, and became in turn a part of the Northwest Territory and the Indiana and Illinois Territories. On December 3, 1818, Illinois entered the Union as the twenty-first state.

In 1842 Abraham Lincoln participated in an episode which embarrassed him the rest of his life although it contributed to the development of his character. During the summer the Whigs attacked the policies of Democratic State Auditor James Shields in a series of letters in the newspaper. Shields, angered by the letter signed Rebecca, learned that Lincoln was the author. When another Aunt Becca letter--actually written by Julia Jayne and Mary Todd, later Lincoln's wife--appeared, shields challenged Lincoln to a duel. Considering the affair absurd, the long-armed Whig chose cavalry broadswords of the largest size and demanded that neither man withdraw farther than eight feet behind a plank set edgewise in the ground. On September 22 the opponents met within three miles of Alton on Missouri soil and settled their differences peacefully.

WOOD RIVER MASSACRE

On July 10, 1814, the "Wood River massacre" took place one-half mile to the north. Here Indians surprised and killed Mrs. Rachel Reagan and six children of the Reagan and Moore families. This was the cruelest of the many Indian depredations which southern Illinois suffered during the War of 1812.

Located: North side of State Rt 140, 75 feet east of Alton State Hospital entrance.

OFFICIAL STATE MAP: K-4
MADISON COUNTY

HALFWAY TAVERN

In 1779 George Rogers Clark led his army from Kaskaskia through this area to Vincennes where they captured Fort Sackville from the British. In 1818 there were several taverns on this section of the Vincennes-St. Louis Trail. Traditionally, the log building to the east was an early haven for travelers.

Location: North side of US 50 about 8½ miles east of Salem in turnout.

Illinois State Historical Library
George Rogers Clark

OFFICIAL STATE MAP: K-7
MARION COUNTY

53

SALEM, ILLINOIS

Salem is locally known as the "Gateway to Little Egypt." Egypt refers to southern Illinois. In the early days of statehood, crop failures threatened the existence of the isolated settlements in northern and central Illinois and trips were made into the more populated southern section of the state to obtain grain. Settlers called such expeditions "going to Egypt," from the Biblical story of the famine.

Salem is located at the crossroads of several prominent old trails, and a settlement was laid out here in 1823. Later Mark Tully and Rufus Ricker deeded the land comprising Salem to Marion County for a county seat. The community grew slowly and in 1855 was legally organized as a town. In 1865 it became a city.

William Jennings Bryan, "the Great Commoner" was born in Salem on March 19, 1860, and lived here until 1883. Newspaperman, congressman, secretary of state, political advisor, and three times a candidate for the presidency. Bryan was considered one of the greatest orators of his day. A well-known lawyer, he served as prosecutor in the famous John Scopes trial shortly before his death in July, 1925. His brithplace at 408 S. Broadway is open to the public.

Salem has a varied agricultural and industrial history. It served as a principal marketplace for red top hayseed which was in great demand in Europe during World War I. Oil was discovered near here in 1938 and reached a production of 259,000 barrels daily in March, 1940. In 1942 Salem became the eastern terminus of a 550 mile petroleum pipeline from Texas.

OFFICIAL STATE MAP K-7
MARION COUNTY

Located: (1) In park in Salem across from the Bryan Memorial on Illinois 37 north. (2) In rest area on Illinois 37, 5 miles south of Salem. (3) At east edge of Salem on the north side of US 50. (4) On south side of US 50, 3½ miles west of Salem.

OFFICIAL STATE MAP: K-7
MARION COUNTY

United Spanish American War veterans in Marion County; soldiers and sailors reunion parade in 1931 in Salem.

William Jennings Bryan after his "Cross of Gold" speech.

Located: Broadway (Ill. 37). Salem.

WILLIAM JENNINGS BRYAN

Lived in Salem, Illinois, from his birth, March 19, 1860, until 1875. A national figure after his "Cross of Gold" speech in 1896, Bryan was the unsuccessful Democratic candidate for President in 1896, 1900, 1908, and served as secretary of state, 1913-1915. He died in 1925 after the Scopes "Evolution" trial.

FORT MASSAC

Here, in 1757, French soldiers erected Fort Ascension. The following year the name was changed to Fort Massac in honor of the Marquis de Massiac, Minister of Marine. In 1778 George Rogers Clark landed here on his historic expedition to the Illinois country. From 1794 to 1812 Fort Massac was occupied by U.S. Regulars.

Located: On US 45 at Fort Massac State Park entrance, east of Metropolis.

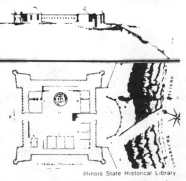

Plat of Ford Massac. The original plan is in the Archives Nationales, Paris.

Located: US 45, ½ mile
north of Brookport.

THY WONDROUS STORY, ILLINOIS

The fertile prairies in Illinois attracted the attention of French trader Louis Jolliet and Father Jacques Marquette as they explored the Mississippi and Illinois Rivers in 1673. France claimed this region until 1763 when she surrendered it to Great Britain by the Treaty of Paris. During the American Revolution George Rogers Clark and his small army scored a bloodless victory when they captured Kaskaskia for the Commonwealth of Virginia, and Illinois became a county of Virginia. This area was ceded to the United States in 1784, and became in turn a part of the Northwest Territory and the Indiana and Illinois territories. On December 3, 1818, Illinois entered the Union as the twenty-first state.

Many of the early settlers came from Kentucky, Tennessee and the southeastern coastal states to live in the southern quarter of Illinois. As the better land was taken up, the line of settlement advanced northward. Within the southern portion of the state, Kaskaskia on the Mississippi River was the terrirorial and the first state capital, and Vandalia was the second state capital.

Eight miles west U.S. 45 passes Fort Massac State Park, a site which the French fortified extensively in 1757. George Rogers Clark entered the Illinois country near it on his way to capture Kaskaskia. The United States used Fort Massac from 1794 until it was finally abandoned in 1814.

Site of Fort Massac.

A PLAN

of the several Villages in the

ILLINOIS COUNTRY,

with Part of the

River Mississippi &c.

by

Tho.s Hutchins,

Captain in the British Army.

(1771)

Scale of Miles.

A plan of Bellefontaine.

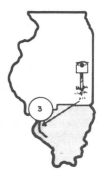

Located: NW corner of Hoener Ave and South Church St. in Waterloo

BELLEFONTAINE

Bellefontaine was one of the first settlements made by Americans in what is now Illinois. The earliest settlers included families of Revolutionary War veterans who had served with George Rogers Clark. Captain James Moore brought a band of pioneers from Virginia and Maryland in the winter of 1781-1782. The settlement took its name from a nearby spring the French called "La Belle Fontaine" (beautiful spring). The 1800 federal census showed that Bellefontaine, with 286 inhabitants, had become the third largest community in the Illinois Territory.

Erected by the monroe county historical society and the illinois state historical society, 1976

DU QUOIN FEMALE SEMINARY

On the hill to the east was the Du Quoin Female Seminary, founded by the Boston Ladies Society for the Promotion of Christian Education.

Later as Du Quoin Academy it was coeducational. The three story brick building, then an orphanage, was closed in 1893. It burned in October, 1898.

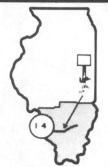

OFFICIAL STATE MAP: M-6
PERRY COUNTY

Located: At old Du Quoin, site of the old Seminary on Ill. 14.

VINCENNES TRAIL

MARKER MISSING

George Rogers Clark with a small band of Kentucky Militiamen, surprised the British garrison at Kaskaskia on July 4, 1778, and forced its surrender. Learning that the British had captured Vincennes, Clark left Kaskaskia for that post early in February, 1779, and passed this way on his march. On February 25, he retook Vincennes thereby breaking the British power in the Illinois country.

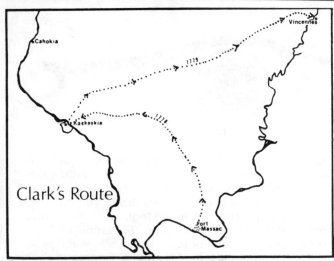

Clark's Route

From: ILLINOIS A HISTORY OF A PRAIRIE STATE by Robert Howard. Used by permission: William B. Erdman's Publishing Co.

Map of Clark's Route.

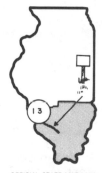

OFFICIAL STATE MAP: M-6
PERRY COUNTY

Located: On State highway 13, one mile south of Coulterville, just over Randolph County line.

Located: Ill. 146, West of Golconda.

John Ross, a Cherokee Chief.

THE CHEROKEE "TRAIL OF TEARS"

During the winter of 1838-1839, some 8,000 Cherokee Indians moved slowly along a route across southern Illinois from Golconda to Jonesboro and south to Cape Girardeau, Missouri. They were being forcibly removed from their improved lands in Georgia, Alabama, North Carolina, and Tennessee to lands in Oklahoma when floating ice on the Mississippi River made further progress difficult. Many died in Illinois during the hard trek. The Cherokees called it their "Trail of Tears."

During Andrew Jackson's administration the movement to remove all Indians to the West gained momentum. A group of Cherokees favorable to removal signed the Treaty of New Echota in Georgia on December 29, 1835, and in the next two years 2,100 cherokees were removed. Chief John Ross and 15,000 followers considered this treaty invalid and remained in the East. On April 6, 1838, President Jackson ordered General Winfield Scott to remove them with troops. The Cherokees asked that they be allowed to direct the march themselves. Scott granted the request.

The first of thirteen detachments left on October 1, 1838, and the others followed within two months. The first group to reach Oklahoma arrived on January 4, 1839, and the last on March 25, 1839. But for nearly three months over one half of the refugees were stranded in southern Illinois. The winter was unusually severe and many settlers were unfriendly. It is estimated that up to 4,000 Cherokees died during the tragic migration. "Trail of Tears" was indeed an appropriate name.

CANTONMENT WILKINSON-VILLE

On the Ohio River three miles south of here Cantonment Wilkinson-Ville, named for Gen. James Wilkinson, was established by Lt. Col. David Strong in 1797 as a post of the United States Army. It was garrisoned until 1804. Here are buried Colonel Strong and scores of soliders who died on duty.

Major General James Wilkinson.

Located: One tenth mile south of road to New Grand Chain on east side Ill. 37.

OFFICIAL STATE MAP O-7
POLASKI COUNTY

Union Gunboat on the Mississippi.

THE MARINE WAYS

During the Civil War the naval depot of the Western River Fleet was located at Mound City. Here the keels of three of the famous Eads ironclad gunboats were laid, and the large force of workmen were employed to keep the fleet in fighting trim. The Marine Ways, still in operation, are 400 yards south of here.

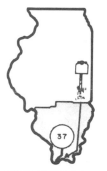

OFFICIAL STATE MAP: P-6
POLASKI COUNTY

Located: East side of Ill. 37, near Intersection of Highway and 4th Streets, Mound City. intersection Main and Central streets.

Located: In Mound City, north side of Ill. 37 - near Intersection Main and Central streets.

UNITED STATES MILITARY HOSPITAL

The southern portion of the brick building at the Ohio levee, 150 yards east of here, was part of a large warehouse which was converted into a military hospital in 1861 and staffed during the Civil War by the Sisters of the Holy Cross. Following the Battle of Shiloh 2200 Union and Confederate wounded were patients there.

Tin Clad 59 and tug boat opposite the Mound City Hospital.

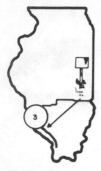

Located: Ill. 3, 3.5 miles
north of Ellis Grove.

THE AMERICAN BOTTOM

"A more congenial soil for general cultivation I believe no where exists, it may be called the Elysium of America." That is how a settler in 1817 described the American Bottom, the lowland between the Mississippi River and the bluffs to the east which stretches from the Wood River to the Kaskaskia. Hundreds of years ago an agricultural people settled in this silt-filled channel of an ancient river and raised crops to feed their large cities. Today many mounds in the area stand as monuments to this early civilization.

The American Bottom served as the center of settlement for the French, the British and finally the Americans in Illinois for over a hundred years. At the height of French activity after 1700 probably no more than 2,000 Frenchmen and Negroes lived in the region but they produced the grain for posts on the Ohio and lower Mississippi, explored the surrounding territory for mineral wealth and established Fort de Chartres.

The British took the land from the French in 1763 but their interest in the American Bottom was slight. When George Rogers Clark led his small army to the area in 1778 he captured Kaskaskia and the other villages without striking a blow. Under the Americans, Kaskaskia became the territorial and the first state capital. Illinois highway maps indicate several parks and memorials between Chester and East St. Louis which will take you back into the intriguing history of the American Bottom.

Illinois State Historical Library

The American Bottom attracted many early pioneers seeking good farm land.

62

Located: I-3, Evansville Road, W. of Schuline.

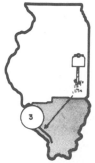

OFFICIAL STATE MAP: M-5
RANDOLPH COUNTY

The Charter Oak School, built in 1873, served as a school until 1953. Its octagonal shape utilizes daylight and offers wind resistance.

CHARTER OAK SCHOOL

Charter Oak School is said to be the only octagonal one-room brick schoolhouse in Illinois. It was built in 1873, in accordance with a design suggested by Daniel Ling, a teacher of the Charter Oak School District. It served as a school until 1953. The octagonal shape utilizes daylight and offers wind resistance. The first school in the district was a log building, erected three years after the Illinois Free School Law was passed in 1845. This was succeeded in 1863 by a frame structure, in which Ling taught in 1872-1873.

Located: Fort Kaskaskia State Park.

FORT KASKASKIA

Fort Kaskaskia, a rectangular wooden stockade, was begun in 1734, completed in 1736, and garrisoned at intervals thereafter by French troops. In 1760 it was rebuilt but in 1764, after the defeat of the French in the French and Indian War, its garrison was withdrawn. Two years later the people of Kaskaskia destroyed the fort to prevent the English from occupying it. For several years during the period of disorder which followed the American Revolution, John Dodge, a notorious adventurer occupied Fort Kaskaskia and made it headquarters for the tyrannical and illegal rule which he maintained over this region. With Dodge's expulsion and the establishment of stable government in 1790, Fort Kaskaskia was abandoned forever.

CHESTER-KASKASKIA, ILLINOIS

Shadrach Bond, first governor of Illinois (1818-1822), is buried in Evergreen Cemetery in Chester. The first recorded settler in the area was John McFerron who purchased land in 1817 but Samuel Smith, who settled here in 1830, is considered the founder of Chester. Formerly known as Smith's Landing, the community was renamed after Chester, England. The town was a river port for the export of such local products as castor oil, flour, and meat during the mid-nineteenth century. It became the county seat in 1848 and was incorporated as a city in 1855.

Kaskaskia, founded in 1703 as a Jesuit mission, became a prominent French village. During the French and Indian War (1754-1763) between France and Britain, Fort Kaskaskia was erected on the bluffs near the settlement. By the Treaty of Paris in 1763, Kaskaskia came under British control. On July 4, 1778 George Rogers Clark captured the Kaskaskia settlement and the area became a part of Virginia. Kaskaskia served as Illinois Territorial capital (1809-1818) and as the first state capital (1818-1820). When the capital was moved to Vandalia, Kaskaskia declined in importance. Mississippi floods from 1844 to 1910 gradually destroyed the old settlement, and the area is now Fort Kaskaskia State Park.

Sites of interest include the Garrison Hill Cemetery containing a monument to the pioneers; the home of Pierre Menard, first lieutenant governor, which is preserved as a state memorial; and the Kaskaskia State Memorial on Kaskaskia Island containing the "Liberty Bell of the West."

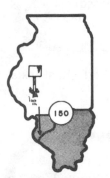

OFFICIAL STATE MAP: M-5
RANDOLPH COUNTY

Located: (1) In rest area on the southeast side of Illinois 150, about two miles northeast of Chester. (2) In rest area on the west side of Illinois 3, two miles south of Ellis Grove, near spur to Fort Kaskaskia State Park. (3) In park in Chester, at toll gate to Mississippi River bridge, Missouri 51 near Illinois 3.

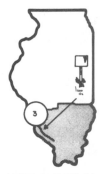

OFFICIAL STATE MAP: M-5
RANDOLPH COUNTY

Illinois State Historical Library View of Kaskaskia from Fort Gage on Garrison Hill, 1893.

FORT DE CHARTRES-PRAIRIE DU ROCHER, ILLINOIS

The fertility of the Mississippi bottom lands in this area attracted settlers early in the eighteenth century. The territory was under French rule and in 1718 Pierre Duque, Sieur de Boisbraint, commandant of the Illinois country, was sent to erect a permanent military post.

The first Fort de Chartres was completed in 1720. Built of wood and exposed to the Mississippi floods, the fort had to be rebuilt in 1727 and 1732. In 1753 construction of a new fort built of stone and farther inland was begun under the direction of Francois Saucier. When it was completed in 1756 it was considered one of the finest forts in North America. The British gained control of the area in 1763 by the Treaty of Paris and in 1765 took possession of the fort which they renamed Fort Cavendish. They destroyed the fort in 1772 when the encroaching Mississippi waters necessitated its abandonment. It had served as the seat of civil and military government in the Illinois country for over half a century. The partially reconstructed fort is a state memorial west on Illinois 155.

Prairie du Rocher, the small French village, four miles east of the fort, was founded in 1722 by Ste. Therese Langlois, nephew of Boisbriant. The Prairie du Rocher Common (land used by all the villagers) was granted to the village by the territorial government in 1743 and was used until 1852. Prairie du Rocher, "Field of the Rock," remains a picturesque village where French Christmas and New Year's customs are still observed.

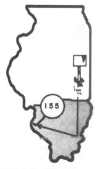

Located: (1) In parking area of Fort de Chartres State Park, off southwest side of Illinois 155.

The powder magazine at Fort Chartres about 1905.

Illinois State Historical Library

Dr. George Fischer was a member of the first and second general assemblies of the Indiana Territory. The territorial Capitol in Vincennes, Indiana is shown above.

DR. GEORGE FISHER

Dr. George Fisher, Kaskaskia physician lived on a farm eight miles west of here from 1806 until his death in 1820. 1801 first sheriff of Randolph County, 1805-1808 member of First and Second General Assemblies of Indiana Territory, 1812-1816 Speaker of House in First and Third General Assemblies of Illinois Territory, 1818 member of First Constitutional Convention.

OFFICIAL STATE MAP: M-5
RANDOLPH COUNTY

Located: Junction of Rts. 3 and 155 at Ruma, Illinois .

Located: At grave site, Ruma, Illinois .

DR. GEORGE FISHER

George Fisher, early Illinois physician, member of the first House of Representatives of Indiana Territory, Speaker of the House in the First and Third Illinois Territorial Assemblies (1812-14, 1816-1818) and member of First Illinois Constitutional Convention in 1818. His body lies here.

HOME OF PIERRE MENARD

This home was built about 1800 by Pierre Menard (1766-1844), presiding officer of the Illinois Territorial Legislature and first Lieutenant Governor. The building is of French colonial architecture. The kitchen contains the original fireplace and water basin, and a rust-red bake oven. The original slave house stands at the rear.

The home of Pierre Menard was built about 1800. The original slave house stands at the rear.

OFFICIAL STATE MAP: M-5
RANDOLPH COUNTY

Located: Ill. 3 In front of the Menard Home State Memorial, northwest of Chester.

Located: On State Rt. 3 at junction with gravel road leading to Fort Kaskaskia State Park, NE corner.

KASKASKIA

From 1703 until it was washed away by the Mississippi two centuries later, the ancient town of Kaskaskia--the second settlement in Illinois, the Territorial capital, and the first state capital--stood two miles southwest of here. Fort Kaskaskia State Park and the Menard Home are memorials to this once-prominent village.

Located: County road BB, near Modoc.

OFFICIAL STATE MAP: M-5
RANDOLPH COUNTY

MODOC ROCK SHELTER

As early as 8000 B.C. prehistoric Indians were camping in the shelter of this great sandstone bluff. These nomadic people, who lived by hunting animals and gathering plants for food and fibers, came here regularly for more than 6000 years. Later Indian groups, who began to settle in villages, used the rock shelter occasionally when hunting. The pioneers and their descendants continued to make use of the shelter in historic times.

LINCOLN AND DOUGLAS IN OLNEY

During the presidential campaign of 1856 Abraham Lincoln and Stephen A. Douglas spoke in Olney at separate political rallies held the same day--Saturday, September 20. In the morning Douglas spoke in a grove near town at a Democratic rally for Buchanan and Breckinridge. In the afternoon Lincoln spoke at the courthouse at a Republican rally for Fremont and Dayton. The Republican speakers--Lincoln, Senator Lyman Trumbull, and Ebenezer Peck of Chicago--also attended the Democratic rally. On the previous day they had challenged the Democrats to a debate, but the Democrats were confident of victory and did not accept.

Located: Ill. 250, Courthouse, Olney.

OFFICIAL STATE MAP: K-9
RICHLAND COUNTY

Illinois State Historical Library

Senator Lyman Trumball who, with Lincoln, challenged the Democrats to a debate in Olney.

OFFICIAL STATE MAP: K-9
RICHLAND COUNTY

Robert Ridgeway. leading American ornithologist. was a founder of the American Ornithologists' Union and contributed greatly to its official checklist of North American Birds published in 1886.

Located: In a turnout on the south side of US 50. one-eighth of a mile south of Olney.

ROBERT RIDGWAY AND "BIRD HAVEN"

Robert Ridgway, leading American ornithologist, was born at Mount Carmel. Illinois on July 2, 1850. As a youth he became interested in birds and sketched many specimens around his home. At the age of seventeen, he was appointed zoologist on a geological survey of the Fortieth Parallel. From 1874 to 1929 he was connected with the Smithsonian Institution first as ornithologist and later as Curator of Birds. He was a founder of the American Ornithologists' Union (1883) and contributed greatly to its official checklist of North American Birds published in 1886. He was a member of the National Academy of Science (1926-1929).

Ridgway published extensively in his field and related areas from 1869 to 1929. His experience with the problems of color and color description in bird portraits resulted in a work entitled **Color Standards and Color Nomenclature** which proved valuable in many fields besides ornithology. He also wrote an authoritative eight-volume study of **The Birds of North and Middle America** published between 1901 and 1919 with two additional volumes in preparation when he died.

In 1916 Ridgway retired to Olney to continue his research at his home which he called Larchmound. He developed an eighteen-acre tract nearby called Bird Haven as a bird sanctuary and experimental area for the cultivation of trees and plants not native to the region. He died at Olney on March 25. 1929. Bird Haven with its variety of trees and birds remains as a memorial to this much-honored American ornithologist. It and Dr. Ridgway's grave are approximately two miles north of here.

STATE
MEMORIAL

Located: South of East St.
Louis, just off Rt. 3.

CAHOKIA COURTHOUSE STATE MEMORIAL

Cahokia Courthouse State Memorial is the oldest house in Illinois, possibly the oldest private dwelling in the midwest and certainly the oldest of all courthouses west of the Allegheny Mountains.

Thought to have been built shortly after 1737, it is an excellent example of the French pioneer log house building with interstices filled with stone and mortar. The walls rest on a foundation of stone nearly two feet thick. The floors are of sassafras puncheons on walnut beams. The roof, of cantilever type, extends down over the porches. The courthouse has four rooms; the courtroom, a jail and probably two offices.

When this building was erected, Cahokia was part of the French province of Louisiana. Marquette and LaSalle failed to stop here; nevertheless, it is the oldest permanent settlement in the Mississippi Valley. It was founded in March 1699 by three missionaries from the Seminary of Foreign Missions of Quebec, Canada. These priests built a chapel dedicated to the Holy Family.

Previously Jesuit priests had traveled this section and for a time they worked side by side with the Seminarians. Finally, the Archbishop of Quebec recognized the Seminarians as sole local representatives of the church and they remained in charge for 65 years.

Cahokia is named for the tribe of Indians that was part of the Illinois Indian Confederation. With their close associates, the Tamoroas, the Cahokias lived in a wooded strip of land between the Mississippi River and Cahokia Creek. They gathered here in the summer for their councils and in the winter ranged the prairies on their great hunts. The word Cahokia signified "wild geese."

Illinois State Historical Library

Cahokia Courthouse, Cahokia, Illinois.

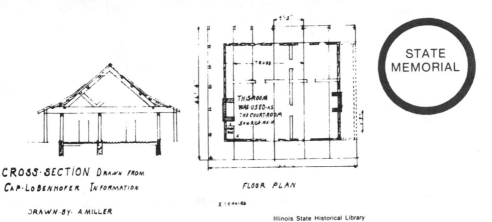

CROSS-SECTION DRAWN FROM CAP-LOBENHOFER INFORMATION

DRAWN BY A MILLER

FLOOR PLAN

X : CHAIRS

Above is a floor plan of the original Cahokia Courthouse thought to have been built shortly after 1737.

The 1732 census showed only 12 white residents, but later it became the most populous of the French Mississippi River towns with over 3,000 residents. Of the half dozen French settlements in this section, Cahokia was the commercial center; Kaskaskia was known for its agriculture and Fort de Chartres was the governmental headquarters. These settlements of white men, with their French customs and government, were surrounded in all directions by miles of Indian country. In Cahokia, as in the other villages, were two distinct communities--one French and one Indian. However, the races mingled in trade and worship and sometimes intermarried. General relations were close and friendly.

As a result of the Seven Year's War of 1756-63, Canada and the Illinois Country were ceded to Great Britain. In 1764 St. Louis was founded four miles north and across the Mississippi River, and many of the Cahokians moved to the new community. They wished to escape the river floods that plagued Cahokia and to live on French soil. They soon regretfully learned that this side of the river had been secretly ceded to Spain by France.

The Cahokia Courthouse was dismantled and moved in 1904 to the grounds of the Louisiana Purchase Exposition in St. Louis as a fair display. At the close of the fair, the building was sold to the Chicago Historical Society. Moved again, a fourth of the original building was set up on the wooded island of Jackson Park in Chicago.

For some time there had been a feeling by many that the courthouse should be returned to its original site. This thought became action with the start of a Cahokia Memorial Survey in 1938. Under the supervision of the Illinois State Museum this project was part of the WPA program.

The excavation of the original site was done under the direction of a state archaeologist during the summer of 1938 and the old stone foundations were uncovered and fragments of ironwork and domestic objects were found.

The reconstruction was made following a searching study of old photographs and sketches of the building, and French buildings of this era in the vicinity, utilizing what material was left of the original building. Artifacts found in excavating and other material dealing with the building are displayed now in the courthouse.

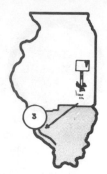

Located: East side of Illinois 3 at the south edge of Cahokia:

CAHOKIA, ILLINOIS

Cahokia, the first permanent white settlement in Illinois in continuous existence, was established in 1699 by priests of the French Seminary of Foreign Missions in Quebec. The site of the Mission of the Holy Family was chosen the previous year by a mission party guided here by the famous explorer Tonti and was adjacent to a village of Tamaroa and Cahokia Indians.

A typical French village gradually grew up around the mission. Its population, always small, was affected by the establishment of Kaskaskia and Fort de Chartres and by the cession of the land to the British in 1765 following the French and Indian War. However, as county seat of St. Clair County, Cahokia at one time was the seat of government for a huge territory which included the 80 northern Illinois counties of today.

Cahokia was not destined to continue in her important position. The recurrent floods of the Mississippi and the growing importance of St. Louis and East St. Louis limited Cahokia. The county seat was removed to Belleville in 1814 and Cahokia became a small agricultural center on the outskirts of East St. Louis.

Yet Cahokia retains her rich heritage. Cahokia Mounds in this vicinity are important remnants of prehistoric Illinois. The famous chief Pontiac was assassinated here in 1769. George Rogers Clark negotiated here for Indian neutrality during the American Revolution. Landmarks such as the Old Church of the Holy Family, the old Cahokia cemetery, the Cahokia Courthouse, and the Jarrot Mansion are representative of Cahokia's proud past.

Illinois State Historical Library

Cahokia shown in the above sketch, was the first permanent white settlement in Illinois.

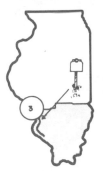

Located: On east side of State Rt. 3 about 200 feet north of St. Route 157, beside "Death of Pontiac" marker.

The Holy Family Church in Cahokia, Illinois.

CAHOKIA

MARKER MISSING

Here, in 1699, priests of the Seminary of Quebec founded the Mission of the Holy Family. Around it developed the village of Cahokia, the first permanent white settlement in Illinois. For more than a century Cahokia prospered, but about 1815 decline commenced, and the village gradually yielded its ancient importance.

CAHOKIA MOUNDS

The Cahokia Mounds represent the most extensive pre-historic Indian remains in the United States. Eighty-five mounds are included in the group, which covers an area of 2000 acres-- The site of successive Indian villages for centuries, these mounds are believed to have been built between 450 and 750 years ago.

Located: U.S. Alt. 40, near Cahokia Mounds State Park.

Cahokia Mounds.

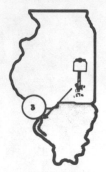

OFFICIAL STATE MAP: L-4
ST. CLAIR COUNTY

Located: East side of State
Rt. 3 beside "Cahokia"
marker.

Pontiac.

Illinois State Historical Library

DEATH OF PONTIAC

In Cahokia, Pontiac, the Ottawa chief who organized the Indian
conspiracy which struck terror along the frontier from 1763 to 1765, met
his death in the early spring of 1769. He was assassinated by a Peoria
Indian after a drunken debauch.

Charles S. Deneen, governor of Illinois from 1905 to 1913, is shown here giving a speech at Lawrenceville.

OFFICIAL STATE MAP: L-5
ST. CLAIR COUNTY

Located: US 50, 303 North Stanton St., Lebanon, west of the McKendree College campus.

THE DENEEN FAMILY

On this site stood the home of the Deneen family long associated with the history of McKendree College -- Rev. William L. Deneen; Professor Samuel H. Deneen; and Charles S. Deneen, governor of Illinois, 1905-1913 and U.S. senator, 1925-1931. They were three generations of outstanding McKendree alumni.

John Mason Peck.

OFFICIAL STATE MAP: L-5
ST. CLAIR COUNTY

Located: On north side US 50, 2.2 miles east of O'Fallon. Erected in front of big tree in front of house.

JOHN MASON PECK

On this site, from 1822 until his death in 1858, lived John Mason Peck, pioneer Baptist preacher, author and educator. Here, in 1827, he founded Rock Springs Seminary. In 1831 the seminary was removed to Alton, where it later became Shurtleff College.

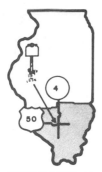

OFFICIAL STATE MAP: L-5
ST. CLAIR COUNTY

Illinois State Historical Library

Located: U.S. 50 & Ill. 4, Lebanon.

"Old Main" on the campus of McKendree College, the oldest college in America.

McKENDREE COLLEGE

Founded at Lebanon in 1828, McKendree College is the oldest college in America under the continuous supervision of the Methodist Church. It was named for Bishop William McKendree. Edward Ames was the first principal, Peter Akers the first president. Present buildings date from 1850.

John Law.

Illinois State Historical Library

OFFICIAL STATE MAP: L-5
ST. CLAIR COUNTY

Located: US 460, 3.2 miles southeast of Freeburg.

THE MISSISSIPPI BUBBLE

"They relate that there are mines of gold and silver. . . .There is reason to believe that the French who will settle among the Illinois Indians will make all these rich discoveries when the colony becomes more thickly populated." Thus John Law, Scot adventurer and gambler, inflated the "Mississippi Bubble" in the fall of 1717. He had convinced the Duke of Orleans, regent for Louis XV, that paper money issued by a national bank and backed by a vast trading and colonizing enterprise would bring new life to the French economy. As part of the scheme, on January 1, 1718, the Company of the West received a 25 year charter to trade, settle and govern in the Mississippi Valley. Speculation in the shares ran wild as Frenchmen of all classes engaged in the fantasy before the bubble burst in 1720 and left many investors bankrupt.

Law's vision of the development of the region required more time and money than he had. Exaggerated accounts attracted some colonists; force brought others. As the operations of the company in lower Louisiana expanded, the district of Illinois profited. Several French villages sprang up in the American Bottom south of here and mining expeditions searched for the fabled minerals. The real wealth in Illinois, however, was the fur trade and the agricultural produce which sustained the other French posts. The company struggled along until Indian warfare and inadequate financial returns forced the surrender of its charter in 1731.

Historic
Site

Illinois State Historical Library

Monk's Mound, one of the Cahokia mounds, in St. Clair County, Illinois.

MONK'S MOUND

Near Cahokia is the largest prehistoric earthwork on the North American continent. 84 other mounds surround it.

The mounds were the work of a group of people who lived along the Illinois, Mississippi, Ohio, Wabash and Tennessee Rivers around 900 A.D.

The temples and houses of their priests were placed on top of the giant mounds.

Monk's Mound, the largest, covers seventeen acres and stands 100 feet high.

From: ILLINOIS A HISTORY OF A PRAIRIE STATE by Robert Howard. Used by permission: William B. Erdman's Publishing Co.

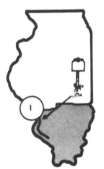

OFFICIAL STATE MAP: L-4
ST. CLAIR COUNTY

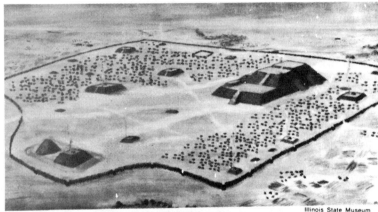

Illinois State Museum

Artist's conception of Monk's Mound, Sand Prairie phase, AD 1250-1500.

Located: Pensoneau-Caillot Pioneer House, 8105-07 Church Lane, East St. Louis.

PENSONEAU-CAILLOT PIONEER HOUSE

Located in the heart of Petit Village Francois, this house was built by Laurent Etienne Pensoneau in 1818. He was the son of Etienne Pensoneau who built the first official St. Clair County Courthouse in 1817. Laurent's bride was a descendant of Jean Baptiste Saucier the designer of the second Fort de Chartres.

THY WONDROUS STORY, ILLINOIS

The fertile prairies in Illinois attracted the attention of French trader Louis Jolliet and Father Jacques Marquette as they explored the Mississippi and Illinois Rivers in 1673. France claimed this region until 1763 when she surrendered it to Great Britain by the Treaty of Paris. During the American Revolution George Rogers Clark and his small army scored a bloodless victory when they captured Kaskaskia for the Commonwealth of Virginia, and Illinois became a county of Virginia. This area was ceded to the United States in 1784, and became in turn a part of the Northwest Territory and the Indiana and Illinois territories. On December 3, 1818, Illinois entered the Union as the twenty-first state.

The Eads Bridge, an engineering achievement of the nineteenth century, spans the Mississippi River from Broadway (East St. Louis) to Washington Avenue (St. Louis). James B. Eads, chief engineer, solved numerous construction problems between August, 1867 and June, 1874.

First, while sinking the foundation on the site of the St. Louis wharf, workmen struck the sunken hulks of three steamboats and four barges. Later, workers in the compressed-air chambers far below the river suffered from the then mysterious "bends." Finally, in the summer of 1873 the steel in the western span expanded in the heat but the arch was closed by packing tons of ice around the metal.

The public doubted the success of the venture until July 2, 1874 when fourteen locomotives crossed back and forth on the bridge in a conclusive test of its strength.

Located: (1) West side of US 50, 1900 ft. southeast of the Junction of US 50 and Ill. 111 in East St. Louis. (2) Us 460, 1 mile southeast of Centreville.

OFFICIAL STATE MAP: K-4
ST. CLAIR COUNTY

Illinois State Historical Library

The Eads Bridge, an engineering achievement of the nineteenth century was finally completed in 1884.

HOMESTEAD OF JUDGE SAMUEL ELDER

Here was located the home of Samuel Elder, cofounder of Elder-Redo now called Eldorado, judge of the county court (1849-1856), school commissioner, collector of Internal Revenue, justice of the peace, and farmer. He and his son, William, together with Joseph and William Reed laid out the village of Eldorado, August 22, 1856.

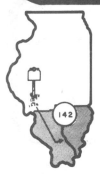

OFFICIAL STATE MAP: N-8
SALINE COUNTY

Located: At Eldorado, under water tower, Ill 142, Broughton Road.

INGERSOLL LAW OFFICE, 1855-1857

Two hundred feet east of here was the Ingersoll law office. Ebon Clark Ingersoll and Robert Green Ingersoll, his younger brother, before they moved to Peoria, had a successful law practice in the Saline County Circuit Court which met in Raleigh, the first county seat of Saline County, 1847-1859.

OFFICIAL STATE MAP: N-8
SALINE COUNTY

Located: In Raleigh on Rt. 126 (junction 34 & 142).

Illinois State Historical Library

Robert Ingersoll and family.

Located: Rt. 142 near southeast Eldorado.

KASKASKIA-SHAWNEETOWN AND GOSHEN TRAILS

In 1816 Congress appropriated $8000 to survey and construct a road from Kaskaskia on the Mississippi to Shawneetown on the Ohio. It became an important east-west thoroughfare for settlers entering the Illinois Territory. At this point the Goshen Trail, which ran from the Goshen settlement near Edwardsville to the Salines, near Equality, joined the Kaskaskia-Shawneetown Trail.

THE TOBACCO INDUSTRY

From the creation of Saline County in 1847 to the end of the century the production of tobacco was the principal industry. In 1870 Saline County had the highest tobacco production in the state.

The Webber brothers of Galatia and Raleigh were the largest buyers and processors in the county, some years exporting 1,500,000 pounds of tobacco.

Located: Ill. 34 at Galatia.

This photo of the Anna State Hospital was taken in about 1905.

Located: (1) In rest area on the south side of Illinois 146, three miles west of Jonesboro. (2) At wye intersection of Illinois 146 and US 51, at the east edge of Anna.

OFFICIAL STATE MAP: O-6
UNION COUNTY

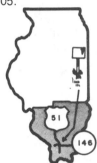

OFFICIAL STATE MAP: O-6
UNION COUNTY

ANNA-JONESBORO

Union County was created on January 2, 1818, by an act of the Territory of Illinois. Two months later, on March 2, 1818, the County Commissioners Court established Jonesboro on land donated by John and Juliet Grammar to serve as county seat. In the 1850's it was decided that the Illinois Central would run through this area. To insure that the railroad would go through the town, Jonesboro was to have a survey made for the railroad. It is said that when the town failed to meet this request, Winstead Davie of Jonesboro submitted a survey routing the railroad through his property east of Jonesboro. A town was established by the railroad and Davie named it Anna in honor of his wife on March 3, 1854.

Jonesboro was the site of the third of the seven Lincoln-Douglas debates on September 15, 1858. Lincoln received a quiet welcome upon his arrival and spent the night before the debate as the guest of D. L. Phillips of Anna. The otherwise uneventful evening was enlivened by the appearance of Donati's Comet. Douglas' arrival was better received than Lincoln's, however the debate was attended by less than 1500 unenthusiastic people—the smallest crowd of the series—and neither man gained ground.

Anna served as one of the nine rendezvous points in Illinois for troops during the Civil War and eight regiments were assembled here. In 1869 the legislature determined to locate the Southern Illinois Hospital for the Insane at Anna. It is now the Anna State Hospital.

Located: (1) East of Dutch Creek Bridge, east of Ware, on Ill. 146, south side, and (2) South side of Ill. 146, 100 yds. east of Dutch Creek Bridge.

OFFICIAL STATE MAP: O-6
UNION COUNTY

CHEROKEE CAMP

During January, 1839, thousands of Cherokee Indians, enroute from Georgia to Indian Territory and unable to cross the Mississippi because of floating ice, camped along Dutch Creek in this vicinity. Unprepared for the intense cold, nearly 2,000 of the 13,000 Indians who started lost their lives during the journey.

LINCOLN-DOUGLAS DEBATE

On September 15, 1858, in the midst of the senatorial campaign of that year, Abraham Lincoln and Stephen A. Douglas met at Jonesboro in the third of the famous series of debates which made Lincoln a national figure. The debate was held in a grove one-quarter mile to the north.

Debate Memorial at Jonesboro.   Illinois State Historical Library

OFFICIAL STATE MAP: O-6
UNION COUNTY

Located: In small circle in center of Jonesboro. State Rt. 146.

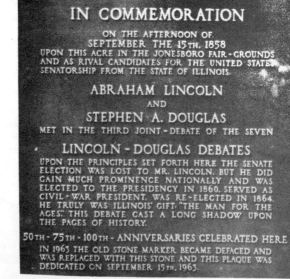

IN COMMEMORATION

ON THE AFTERNOON OF
SEPTEMBER THE 15TH, 1858
UPON THIS ACRE IN THE JONESBORO FAIR-GROUNDS
AND AS RIVAL CANDIDATES FOR THE UNITED STATES
SENATORSHIP FROM THE STATE OF ILLINOIS.

ABRAHAM LINCOLN
AND
STEPHEN A. DOUGLAS
MET IN THE THIRD JOINT-DEBATE OF THE SEVEN

LINCOLN - DOUGLAS DEBATES
UPON THE PRINCIPLES SET FORTH HERE THE SENATE
ELECTION WAS LOST TO MR. LINCOLN, BUT HE DID
GAIN MUCH PROMINENCE NATIONALLY AND WAS
ELECTED TO THE PRESIDENCY IN 1860, SERVED AS
CIVIL-WAR PRESIDENT, WAS RE-ELECTED IN 1864.
HE TRULY WAS ILLINOIS' GIFT "THE MAN FOR THE
AGES". THIS DEBATE CAST A LONG SHADOW UPON
THE PAGES OF HISTORY.

50TH - 75TH - 100TH - ANNIVERSARIES CELEBRATED HERE
IN 1963 THE OLD STONE MARKER BECAME DEFACED AND
WAS REPLACED WITH THIS STONE AND THIS PLAQUE WAS
DEDICATED ON SEPTEMBER 15TH, 1963.

OFFICIAL STATE MAP: O-6
UNION COUNTY

Located: Ill. 146, west of Jonesboro.

Winfield Scott.

THE CHEROKEE "TRAIL OF TEARS"

During the winter of 1838-1839, some 8,000 Cherokee Indians moved slowly along a route across southern Illinois from Golconda to Jonesboro and south to Cape Girardeau, Missouri. They were being forcibly removed from their improved lands in Georgia, Alabama, North Carolina, and Tennessee to lands in Oklahoma when floating ice on the Mississippi River made further progress difficult. Many died in Illinois during the hard trek. The Cherokees called it their "Trail of Tears."

During Andrew Jackson's administration the movement to remove all Indians to the West gained momentum. A group of Cherokees favorable to removal signed the Treaty of New Echota in Georgia on December 29, 1835, and in the next two years 2,100 Cherokees were removed. Chief John Ross and 15,000 followers considered this treaty invalid and remained in the East. On April 6, 1838, President Jackson ordered General Winfield Scott to remove them with troops. The Cherokees asked that they be allowed to direct the march themselves. Scott granted the request.

The first of thirteen detachments left on October 1, 1838, and the others followed within two months. The first group to reach Oklahoma arrived on January 4, 1839, and the last on March 25, 1839. But for nearly three months over one half of the refugees were stranded in southern Illinois. The winter was unusually severe and many settlers were unfriendly. It is estimated that up to 4,000 Cherokees died during the tragic migration. "Trail of Tears" was indeed an appropriate name.

THY WONDROUS STORY, ILLINOIS

The fertile prairies in Illinois attracted the attention of French trader Louis Jolliet and Father Jacques Marquette as they explored the Mississippi and Illinois Rivers in 1673. France claimed this region until 1763 when she surrendered it to Great Britain by the Treaty of Paris. During the American Revolution George Rogers Clark and his small army scored a bloodless victory when they captured Kaskaskia for the Commonwealth of Virginia, and Illinois became a county of Virgnia. This area was ceded to the United States in 1784, and became in turn a part of the Northwest Territory and the Indiana and Illinois territories. On December 3, 1818, Illinois entered the Union as the twenty-first state.

If you had been traveling through this area early in the nineteenth century you might have seen bands of Indians following the trail from Shawneetown to Vincennes which skirted the west side of the Wabash River. Or, if you had been driving between Mt. Carmel and Carmi on September 2, 1840, you might have seen two men and a girl bouncing in a one-seated buggy as they headed north. The tall, thin man, Abraham Lincoln, was campaigning in the area for the Whig presidential candidate, William Henry Harrison.

Early in this century pearl fishing along the Wabash River in this county proved lucrative. From April to October farmers, clerks, mechanics, rivermen and laborers rushed to the fresh-water mussel beds. Before the supply was exhausted they took an estimated million dollars in pearls from the river.

Located: Illinois 1, just south of Mt. Carmel.

Illinois State Historical Library

Hanging Rock, Wabash River, near Mt. Carmel, Illinois.

OFFICIAL STATE MAP: L-10
WABASH COUNTY

OFFICIAL STATE MAP: L-10
WABASH COUNTY

Located: West side of
Illinois 1, 3¼ miles north of
Mt. Carmel.

Anthony Wayne.

THY WONDROUS STORY, ILLINOIS

The fertile prairies in Illinois attracted the attention of French trader Louis Jolliet and Father Jacques Marquette as they explored the Mississippi and Illinois Rivers in 1673. France claimed this region until 1763 when she surrendered it to Great Britain by the Treaty of Paris. During the American Revolution George Rogers Clark and his small army scored a bloodless victory when they captured Kaskaskia for the Commonwealth of Virginia, and Illinois became a county of Virginia. This area was ceded to the United States in 1784, and became in turn a part of the Northwest Territory and the Indiana and Illinois territories. On December 3, 1818, Illinois entered the Union as the twenty-first state.

In August, 1795, Anthony Wayne signed the Treaty of Greenville which provided for the first cession of land in Illinois from the Indians to the United States. There were five specific areas in Illinois under this treaty and one, the Vincennes Tract, included this site.

The treaty could not guarantee peace and the settlers erected forts and blockhouses throughout Wabash County. Four miles to the northeast this highway passes the site of one of the largest stockades in this area, Fort Compton, which was built in 1810.

From 1814 to 1817 Edwards County stretched from the Wabash River to about U.S. 51, and from its present southern boundary to the Canadian border. Palmyra, the county seat for this immense territory was about two miles south of this site on the Wabash River.

Morris Birkbeck.

Located: North side of Illinois 15, 4¼ miles west of Mount Carmel.

THY WONDROUS STORY, ILLINOIS

The fertile prairies in Illinois attracted the attention of French trader Louis Jolliet and Father Jacques Marquette as they explored the Mississippi and Illinois Rivers in 1673. France claimed this region until 1763 when she surrendered it to Great Britain by the Treaty of Paris. During the American Revolution George Rogers Clark and his small army scored a bloodless victory when they captured Kaskaskia for the Commonwealth of Virginia, and Illinois became a county of Virginia. This area was ceded to the United States in 1784, and became in turn a part of the Northwest Territory and the Indiana and Illinois territories. On December 3, 1818, Illinois entered the Union as the twenty-first state.

Communities in this area have a varied historic background. Mt. Carmel was established in 1817 by three Methodist ministers who wanted to found a town based on a strict civil and moral code. The first brick church in the state was built here in 1824. Above Mt. Carmel on the Wabash is the site of Palmyra, seat of Edwards County when it included over one third of the state. Removal of the county seat and Palmyra's unhealthy location caused its abandonment by 1828. Only a commerative plaque remains today.

Highway 15 passes through Albion, center of the English settlement established in 1818 by Morris Birkbeck and George Flower. The first Moravian Church in Illinois, built in 1845, is located at West Salem. William E. Borah, United States Senator from Idaho, was born in 1865 near Fairfield.

Illinois Agricultural College.

OFFICIAL STATE MAP: L-6
WASHINGTON COUNTY

Located: US 51, In Irvington
Park, Irvington.

ILLINOIS AGRICULTURAL COLLEGE

Illinois Agricultural College at Irvington was the first college in the state for instruction in scientific and practical agricultural methods. It was chartered by the Illinois General Assembly in 1861 and opened in 1866. The main buildings were southwest of here on 560 acres of farmland. Almost from its beginning, the school encountered financial difficulties. In 1878 title to the college and land was vested in the state of Illinois. The property was sold and the proceeds given to Southern Illinois Normal University. Irvington College and the Hudelson Baptist Orphanage, 1907-1936, later occupied the campus.

CARMI, ILLINOIS

On December 9, 1815, the General Assembly of the Illinois Territory created White County out of the northern section of Gallatin County. Settlers had been in the area for almost a decade before Carmi was platted as the seat of the new county in 1816 when Captain Leonard White, veteran of the War of 1812 for whom the county was named, James Ratcliff, Daniel Hay, Willis Hargrave, and four other men came here from Equality. Lowry Hay and White were joint proprietors of Carmi, and Hay selected for the community the name which can be traced back to the Biblical character who was a son of Reuben, nephew of Joseph, and grandson of Jacob.

The residence of John Craw served as White County's first courthouse. It later became the home of John M. Robinson (1794-1843), who served as U.S. Senator from Illinois (1831-1843) and was a justice on the Illinois Supreme Court (1843). Carmi was also the home of four members of the U.S. House of Representatives: Colonel John M. Crebs (1868-1873), James Robert Williams (1889-1894, 1899-1905), Orlando Burrell (1895-1897), and Roy Clippinger (1945-1949).

Other sites of historical interest in Carmi include the Ratcliff Inn, where Abraham Lincoln stayed in 1840 while campaigning for Whig presidential candidate William Henry Harrison and which was restored in 1960 by the White County Historical Society, and the house built in 1871 by Colonel Everton J. Conger, commander of the troops which captured John Wilkes Booth, Lincoln's assassin. Historical markers have been erected on these sites.

Located: (1) On private property on the south side of US 460, five miles west of Carmi. (2) On private property on the east side of Illinois 1, at the south edge of Carmi. (3) On the east side of Illinois 1, two miles north of Carmi.

OFFICIAL STATE MAP: M-9
WHITE COUNTY

OFFICIAL STATE MAP: M-9
WHITE COUNTY

Illinois State Historical Library

The old White County Courthouse in Carmi.

Located: County road, southeast of Carmi.

BIG PRAIRIE CHURCH
ESTABLISHED 1812

This church was the cradle of Methodism in White County. Early pioneers risked Indian raids to worship in the cabins of Robert Land and John Hanna. In 1812 presiding elder Peter Cartwright sent circuit rider John Smith to this settlement. This church was organized in Hanna's house.

Illinois State Historical Library

This photo on memory plate is the oldest house in Carmi. It was built in 1815 and later purchased by General John M. Robinson.

Located: 110 South Main Cross Street, Carmi.

CARMI'S OLDEST HOUSE

This house was built by early settler John Craw prior to 1817. In 1835 it was purchased by John M. Robinson, US senator (1831-43) and Illinois Supreme Court justice (1843). The house was later occupied by his daughter Mrs. Robert Stewart and his granddaughter Miss Mary Jane Stewart.

Illinois State Historical Library

Located: 302 West Main Street, Carmi.

Conger House.

COLONEL CONGER HOUSE

Colonel Everton J. Conger, who commanded the troops capturing Abraham Lincoln's assassin, John Wilkes Booth, built this house in 1871. He practiced law in Carmi, became a Federal judge in Montana Territory, and later moved to Hawaii where he was an advisor to Queen Liliuokalani. The house was remodeled in 1941.

THE FIRST PRESBYTERIAN CHURCH IN ILLINOIS

In 1816 the Reverend James McGready of Kentucky organized Sharon, the first Presbyterian Church in Illinois, with Peter Miller, James Mayes and James Rutledge as ruling Elders. Three miles northeast of this site B. F. Spilman, active Presbyterian Church organizer, was ordained in 1824; ½ mile east is the present building and the 1817 cemetery.

Illinois State Historical Library

Located: Three miles south of U.S. 460 on U.S. 45.

First Presbyterian Church.

Located: 312 South First Street. Carmi.

"FLOW GENTLY, SWEET AFTON"

The music for this song was composed by Jonathan Edwards Spilman in 1836. He entered the ministry in 1858 and became pastor of the first Presbyterian Church in 1881. This church had been organized by his brother Benjamin F. Spilman on November 25, 1827, and was the first church in Carmi.

LIBERTY'S PIONEER MILL

This mill, started in 1833 by Andrew Smith, was continued by his descendants, the Morrison family, until 1864. The flint mill stones, imported from France, have been grinding corn since 1859. The town, named Liberty by Scotch pioneers who settled here around 1810, was later renamed Burnt Prairie.

Liberty's Pioneer Mill.

Located: County road to Grayville, Burnt Prairie.

The Ratcliff Inn was erected in 1828 by James Ratcliff, a founder of Carmi.

OFFICIAL STATE MAP: M-9
WHITE COUNTY

Located: Main Street, Carmi.

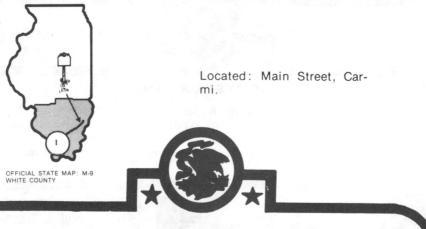

RATCLIFF INN

This building was erected in 1828 by James Ratcliff. Nicknamed "Old Beaver" because of his energy, he was a founder of Carmi (1816), an inn-keeper, merchant, and postmaster, and White County's first clerk, recorder, and probate judge. Abraham Lincoln lodged here in 1840. The inn was restored in 1960.

SOUTHERN ILLINOIS COLLEGE

Alma mater of United States Senators William E. Borah, Idaho, and Wesley L. Jones, Washington. This educational institution was chartered by the Cumberland Presbyterian Church (1873). From the 1890's until 1935 it was a public school. It was purchased for use as a community center by the Kiwanis Club and Enfield citizens in 1967.

Located: U.S. 45, Enfield.

OFFICIAL STATE MAP: M-8
WHITE COUNTY

Southern Illinois College, about 1883.

Illinois State Historical Library

THY WONDROUS STORY, ILLINOIS

The fertile prairies in Illinois attracted the attention of French trader Louis Jolliet and Father Jacques Marquette as they explored the Mississippi and Illinois Rivers in 1673. France claimed this region until 1763 when she surrendered it to Great Britain by the Treaty of Paris. During the American Revolution George Rogers Clark and his small army scored a bloodless victory when they captured Kaskaskia for the Commonwealth of Virginia, and Illinois became a county of Virginia. This area was ceded to the United States in 1784, and became in turn a part of the Northwest Territory and the Indiana and Illinois territories. On December 3, 1818, Illinois entered the Union as the twenty-first state.

Many of the early settlers came from Kentucky, Tennessee and the southeastern coastal states to live in the southern quarter of Illinois. As the better land was taken up, the line of settlement advanced northward. In the southern portion of the state, Kaskaskia on the Mississippi River was the territorial and the first state capital, and Vandalia was the second state capital.

Southern Illinois has attracted travelers for many years. In 1822 an Englishman riding from Carmi to New Harmony reported that the road "passes through the low grounds, or as they are called, 'the Flats' of the Big Wabash. The lands of the river bottoms, or flats, throughout the whole of the United States, are always reckoned very rich and productive, and those of the Wabash are particularly so."

OFFICIAL STATE MAP: M-9
WHITE COUNTY

Located: North side of US 460, 4½ miles west of the Indiana state line near Crossville.

Illinois State Historical Library

Many pioneers were forced to return home penniless after emigrating to the West, but that did not stop others from trying their luck in the new land.

THE
PLAINS

OFFICIAL STATE MAP: H-1
ADAMS COUNTY

From: FROM SLAVE TO PRIEST by Sr. Caroline Hemesath, 1973

Father Tolton.

Located: 7th   &   Maine,
Quincy.

AUGUSTINE TOLTON

Father Tolton, the first Negro priest in the United States, was born of slave parents in Brush Creek, Missouri, in 1854. Educated at Quincy schools, he returned to this city after his ordination in Rome Italy, in 1886. He celebrated his first public mass at St. Boniface Church. He became pastor of St. Joseph Church in Quincy and later established St. Monica's Church for Negroes in Chicago. He died in Chicago in 1897, and is buried at St. Peter's Cemetery, Quincy.

Located: East side of US
24, 2½ miles north of
Quincy.

THY WONDROUS STORY, ILLINOIS

The fertile prairies in Illinois attracted the attention of French trader Louis Jolliet and Father Jacques Marquette as they explored the Mississippi and Illinois Rivers in 1673. France claimed this region until 1763 when she surrendered it to Great Britain by the Treaty of Paris. During the American Revolution George Rogers Clark and his small army scored a bloodless victory when they captured Kaskaskia for the Commonwealth of Virginia, and Illinois became a county of Virginia. This area was ceded to the United States in 1784, and became in turn a part of the Northwest Territory and the Indiana and Illinois territories. On December 3, 1818, Illinois entered the Union as the twenty-first state.

U. S. 24 leaves Quincy, site of the sixth debate between Abraham Lincoln and Stephen A. Douglas in 1858, and between the Mississippi and Illinois Rivers cuts diagonally across the Military Tract, an area used as bounty land for veterans of the War of 1812. This highway passes the ancient Indian burial site at Dickson Mounds State Memorial near Lewistown and the state park, south of the Illinois River Bridge in Peoria, where French explorer Sieur De LaSalle built Fort Crevecoeur in 1680.

Between the Illinois River and the eastern border of the state, U. S. 24 cuts across the prairies where after 1835 the cattle kings fattened large herds for sale in the eastern markets. As late as the 1880's the Corn Belt maintained more cattle than the Great Plains.

Dickson Mounds archaeological site near Lewistown.   Illinois State Historical Library

99

OFFICIAL STATE MAP: H-3
BROWN COUNTY

James W. Singleton.

Illinois State Historical Library

Location: U.S. 24, 6 miles
east of Mt. Sterling

MT. STERLING, ILLINOIS

In 1824 Cornelius Vandeventer, a native of Ohio, became the first permanent settler in this area. Additional pioneers came over the next few years from Kentucky, Tennessee, Virginia, and North Carolina. In 1829 Alexander Curry purchased a claim on the site of the future Mt. Sterling. Curry and his family laid out the town in 1834. At that time, this area formed the southern part of Schuyler County. Two years later, attempts were made to move the county seat from Rushville to a location nearer to the center of the county. When these failed, Brown County, named after General Jacob Brown, a veteran of the War of 1812, was created on February 1, 1839. Mt. Sterling was named the county seat the same year. It was on a major route of the western migration beginning in 1849 with the discovery of gold in California.

James Washington Singleton came to this area from Virginia around 1834 and lived in Mt. Sterling until 1854 when he moved to Quincy. A doctor, lawyer, and later a railroad executive, he became a brigadier general in the Illinois militia and served in the "Mormon War" in 1844. He was also a delegate to two Illinois state constitutional conventions, a member of the Illinois legislature, and a member of the U.S. Congress.

Stephen A. Douglas held court in Mt. Sterling in 1841-1843 while circuit court judge. Abraham Lincoln spoke here on October 19, 1858 while campaigning for the office of U.S. Senator.

Illinois State Historical Library

Dr. Charles Chandler about 1850.

Located: (1) Ill. 78, Jacksonville and Havana Railroad, Chandlerville. (2) Chandlerville-Oakford road, Chandlerville.

OFFICIAL STATE MAP: H-4
CASS COUNTY

CHANDLERVILLE

Founded 1832 by Dr. Charles Chandler of Rhode Island.

VIRGINIA

County seat of Cass County. Founded 1836 by Dr. H. H. Hall.

  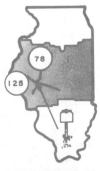

OFFICIAL STATE MAP: H-4
CASS COUNTY

OFFICIAL STATE MAP: H-4
CASS COUNTY

OFFICIAL STATE MAP: H-4
CASS COUNTY

Located: (1) Intersection Ill. 125 and Ill. 78 in front of Cass Consumer Service, Inc., Virginia. (2) North side Ill. 125 on property of Glenn Birnbaum, Virginia. (3) US 67 on line between Sudbrink and Kerry property, Virginia. (4) North side US 67 north of Virginia on Kerry's Farm Supply property, Virginia.

Illinois State Historical Library

French Trader Louis Jolliet who, with Father Jacques Marquette, explored the Mississippi and Illinois Rivers in 1673.

Located: South side of US 40. 1.5 miles west of the Indiana state line near Marshall.

THY WONDROUS STORY, ILLINOIS

SEE HISTORIC ILLINOIS

The fertile prairies in Illinois attracted the attention of French trader Louis Jolliet and Father Jacques Marquette as they explored the Mississippi and Illinois rivers in 1673. France claimed this region until 1763 when she surrendered it to Great Britain by the Treaty of Paris. During the American Revolution George Rogers Clark and his small army scored a bloodless victory when they captured Kaskaskia for the Commonwealth of Virginia, and Illinois became a county of Virginia. This area was ceded to the United States in 1784, and became in turn a part of the Northwest Territory and the Indiana and Illinois territories. On December 3, 1818, Illinois entered the Union as the twenty-first state.

Seven years earlier the National Road began in the east and gradually pushed west as a major route for emigrants, freight wagons and stage coaches. Surveyors marked the route from this point to Vandalia in 1828 and construction in Illinois, limited by Congress to grading and bridging, began. The road was a track of dust or mud around ungrubbed trees and, as an English traveler found in 1842, deep holes in the center of the roadbed from which a settler had taken clay for his chimney.

Early in the twentieth century the development of the automobile led to demands for better roads. The National Road became a part of the cross-country National Old Trails Road, now U.S. 40, and was marked by red, white and blue bands on wayside posts.

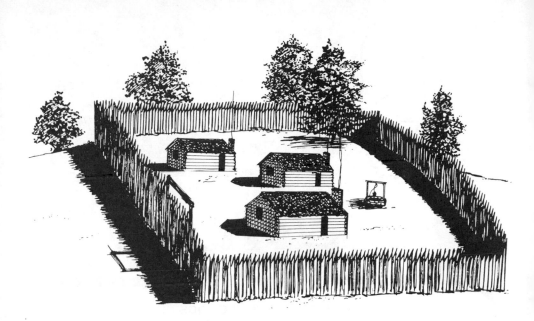

OFFICIAL STATE MAP: J-10
CLARK COUNTY

Located: In park, West Union.

FORT HANDY

Fort Handy, built in 1816, was located 1200 feet southeast of this park on a knoll. The fort, the only structure of its kind in Clark County, was built by the family of Thomas Handy and contained three cabins and a well surrounded by a bulletproof palisade.

Located: Ill. 49. Lincoln Heritage Trail. E. of West-field.

MARGARETTA POST OFFICE

On this site stood Margaretta Post Office, which served many northwestern communities of Clark County from 1840 to 1861. It was named for Margaret. wife of the postmaster, William B. Marrs. Mail was carried to the post office first in saddlebags by horseback and later in portmanteaus by stagecoach. Marrs was a representative in the state legislature, 1836-1837. He was also a justice of the peace, 1835-1837, and a supervisor of roads in 1842.

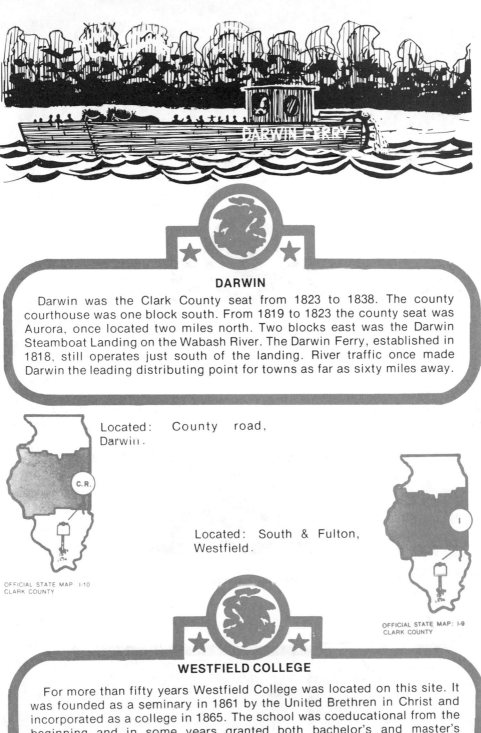

DARWIN

Darwin was the Clark County seat from 1823 to 1838. The county courthouse was one block south. From 1819 to 1823 the county seat was Aurora, once located two miles north. Two blocks east was the Darwin Steamboat Landing on the Wabash River. The Darwin Ferry, established in 1818, still operates just south of the landing. River traffic once made Darwin the leading distributing point for towns as far as sixty miles away.

Located: County road, Darwin.

OFFICIAL STATE MAP I-10
CLARK COUNTY

Located: South & Fulton, Westfield.

OFFICIAL STATE MAP: I-9
CLARK COUNTY

WESTFIELD COLLEGE

For more than fifty years Westfield College was located on this site. It was founded as a seminary in 1861 by the United Brethren in Christ and incorporated as a college in 1865. The school was coeducational from the beginning and in some years granted both bachelor's and master's degrees. Its peak enrollment, reached in 1909, was 160. It closed in June 1914. Three years later the old college building, then being used by Westfield Township High School, was destroyed by fire.

Illinois State Historical Library

This early drawing shows Lincoln on a trip to New Orleans visiting the slave market.

Located: Rutherford home, Oakland.

HOME OF DR. HIRAM RUTHERFORD

This was the home of Dr. Hiram Rutherford, who was involved in 1847 in a case in which Abraham Lincoln represented a slaveholder. Rutherford and Gideon Ashmore harbored a family of slaves who had sought their help. The slaves belonged to Robert Matson, a Kentuckian, who had brought them north to work on his farm. While the slaves were being sheltered in Ashmore's Tavern, Matson obtained a court order to have the slaves jailed. Rutherford and Ashmore sued out a writ of Habeas Corpus for their release. Matson then hired Lincoln. The Circuit Court, after a hearing, freed the slaves.

Located: On north-south oiled road at junction of dirt road extending east to farm, south of Farmington.

THE LAST LINCOLN FARM

In 1837 Thomas Lincoln erected a cabin on a tract of land situated one-half mile to the east. Here he resided until his death in 1851. Abraham Lincoln visited here frequently, and after 1841 held title to forty acres of land on which his parents lived. The State of Illinois now owns most of the Lincoln farm.

House in which Thomas Lincoln. the president's father. died near Charleston, Ill. Illinois State Historical Library

106

LINCOLN-DOUGLAS DEBATE

On September 18, 1858, the fourth of the famous joint debates between Abraham Lincoln and Stephen A. Douglas was held approximately one-quarter mile south of here. Twelve thousand people heard the two candidates for the United States senatorship discuss the question of slavery in American politics.

Located: On south side of State Route 16 at western edge of Charleston (north of fair grounds), 75-100 feet east of Big Four tracks.

OFFICIAL STATE MAP I-9
COLES COUNTY

Illinois State Historical Library

Artist's interpretation of the Lincoln- Douglas debate in Charleston.

LINCOLN FARM, 1831-1834

From 1831 to 1834 Thomas and Sarah Lincoln, father and stepmother of Abraham Lincoln, lived in a cabin which stood a short distance to the north. It was their first home in Coles County, and their second home in Illinois.

OFFICIAL STATE MAP I-9
COLES COUNTY

Located: On north side of Lincoln National Memorial Highway county road. E-W county road ½ mile north of Lerna Road - Sec. 5, R8E, T11N.

Illinois State Historical Library

Grave of Thomas and Sarah Lincoln.

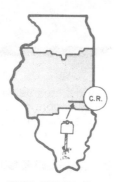

OFFICIAL STATE MAP I-9
COLES COUNTY

Illinois State Historical Library

Located: On south side of Lincoln National Memorial Highway, about 1 mile SW of Lerna. Sec. 9 or 10, T 12 N R8E .

Sarah Bush Lincoln, stepmother of Abraham Lincoln.

LINCOLN FARM, 1834-1837

In 1834 Thomas Lincoln purchased 40 acres situated about 400 yards north and east of this point. Here, with his wife Sarah, he lived until 1837, when he sold the land. It was his second home in Coles County.

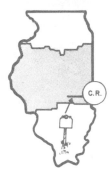

OFFICIAL STATE MAP I-9
COLES COUNTY

Located: At Moore house, south of Charleston on Lincoln National Memorial Highway.

MOORE HOUSE

Here on January 31, 1861, President-elect Abraham Lincoln visited his stepmother Mrs. Sarah Bush Lincoln and her daughter Mrs. Reuben Moore (Matilda Johnston). This was his last visit to Coles County before leaving Illinois for his inauguration. Mrs. Lincoln returned with him to Charleston that night and their farewells were said the next morning.

Moore House.

Illinois State Historical Library

Located: At or near en-
trance to cemetery. About
1½ miles SW of Campbell -
Sec. 19, R8E, T11N.

SHILOH CEMETERY

In Shiloh Cemetery are the graves of Thomas and Sarah Lincoln, father
and stepmother of Abraham Lincoln. On January 31, 1861, shortly before
assuming the presidency, Lincoln came here from Springfield to visit his
father's grave in company with his stepmother.

ULYSSES S. GRANT
IN MATTOON

On May 15, 1861, Ulysses S. Grant mustered in the Seventh District
Regiment in Mattoon. As recruiting officer, Grant had neither uniform nor
commission. A month later, as a colonel, Grant took command of the
group, renamed the 21st Illinois Volunteer Infantry Regiment. Of the 1,250
original enlistees, 603 marched with Grant into battle.

Located: 18th & Prairie,
Mattoon.

Illinois State Historical Library

An early picture of U. S. Grant during the Civil
War.

Illinois State Historical Library

Log Cabin built by Abraham Lincoln and his father in 1831, in Coles County, Ill.: Taken to Chicago during the World's Fair by the Abraham Lincoln Log Cabin Association. West room showing fire place and cooking utensils: spinning wheel used by Abraham Lincoln's mother.

OFFICIAL STATE MAP: I-8
COLES COUNTY

Located: Lincoln Log Cabin
State Park.

SITE OF THE LINCOLN CABIN

The Lincoln cabin stood approximately 200 feet north of this point.

111

PARIS, ILLINOIS

Paris lies in the heart of a rich farming area. Most of the land embraced in Edgar County, including Paris, remained Kickapoo hunting grounds until 1819, but the eastern quarter of the county was part of a tract ceded by the Indians in 1819 and offered for sale at Vincennes as early as 1816. Edgar County was established in 1823, and Paris was laid out on twenty-six acres donated by Samuel Vance in April of that year. The Edgar County Courthouse is located at the center of the parcel of land.

Alone or with others, Vance laid out the earliest roads from Paris in 1823-1824. The first road, later known as the Lower Terre Haute Road, is still being traveled today. A second road ran to Darwin, in Clark County, and another road ran to Marshall, now the seat of Clark County. The fourth road, to the Vermilion salines near Danville, formed part of the Vincennes Trace and is now a section of Illinois Route 1 to Chicago.

At 130 South Central Avenue in Paris is the former home of Milton K. Alexander, brigadier general in the Illinois Mounted Volunteers during the Black Hawk War of 1832. The house was built in 1826 and enlarged in 1840. Alexander was acquainted with Abraham Lincoln, who as a lawyer frequently came to Parish when Edgar County was in the Eighth Judicial Circuit.

Lincoln spoke in Paris on August 6, 1856, on behalf of the Republican presidential candidate, John C. Fremont. Lincoln spoke in Paris again on September 7, 1858, in his unsuccessful campaign against Stephen A. Douglas for the United States Senate. A large proportion of the early settlers in Paris were from the South, and during the Civil War, there were many southern sympathizers called Copperheads. Some of these people were defeated in a minor clash with Union troops in February 1864.

M. K. Alexander.

Located: Kiwanis Park, west side of Ill. 1, at north end of Paris.

OFFICIAL STATE MAP: J-10
EDGAR COUNTY

112

OFFICIAL STATE MAP: H-10
EDGAR COUNTY

Located: West side of Illinois 1, 2.4 miles north of Chrisman.

Illinois State Historical Library

This map shows the French settlement in the Illinois country at the time of Croghan's expedition in 1765.

PONTIAC PEACE TREATY

A few miles west of here on July 18, 1765, Pontiac, an Ottawa chief, and George Croghan, British representative, met in a formal peace council which ended the most threatening Indian uprising against the British in North America. Following the French and Indian War (1754-1763), many Indian tribes showed dissatisfaction with British rule. Indian leaders believed the land belonged to the Indians and that the French and British occupied it only by their consent, but the British had no intention of accepting Indian tribes as independent national units possessing sovereignty. This disagreement and others concerning liquor, ammunition, and other gifts led to open hostilities.

On May 3, 1763, Pontiac led the Ottawa and other tribes in an attack on Fort Detroit. Additional tribes attacked other forts. Soon the frontier was the scene of an extensive Indian uprising. By August, only Detroit, Fort Pitt, and Fort Niagara remained in British hands. Pontiac held his followers to a six months siege of Detroit which was remarkable as warriors preferred active combat. Contemporary estimates of the number killed or captured by the Indians ran as high as 2,000, but the actual figure was closer to 600.

The siege failed and Pontiac traveled west to seek French aid. When this was refused, Pontiac agreed to meet the English representative George Croghan. Following this meeting, Pontiac accompanied Croghan to Detroit where they arrived on August 17, 1765, to finalize the treaty with appropriate ceremonies.

OFFICIAL STATE MAP H-10
EDGAR COUNTY

Located: US 150 turnout,
just west of the Indiana line.

THY WONDROUS STORY, ILLINOIS

SEE
HISTORIC
ILLINOIS

The fertile prairies in Illinois attracted the attention of French trader Louis Jolliet and Father Jacques Marquette as they explored the Mississippi and Illinois Rivers in 1673. France claimed this region until 1763 when she surrendered it to Great Britain by the Treaty of Paris. During the American Revolution George Rogers Clark and his small army scored a bloodless victory when they captured Kaskakia for the Commonwealth of Virginia, and Illinois became a county of Virginia. This area was ceded to the United States in 1784, and became in turn a part of the Norhtwest Territory and the Indiana and Illinois territories. On December 3, 1818, Illinois entered the Union as the twenty-first state.

Two extensive livestock farms were located in Edgar County. At their height around 1875, each farm consisted of several thousand acres on which up to 1,000 shorthorn cattle were fattened yearly for market until they weighed up to 3,000 pounds apiece.

These farms were representative of a phenomena extending across Illinois in the third quarter of the nineteenth century. The "Cattle Kings in the Prairies" were men who early recognized the value of this land, purchased thousands of acres, and used it to fatten livestock for midwestern and eastern markets. Agricultural changes eventually caused them to de-emphasize livestock feeding and to rent the land to grain farming tenants. However, the cattle kings retained ownership and remained wealthy, powerful, and influential. Some were active in state and national politics. Their descendants still own some of the tracts.

THY WONDROUS STORY, ILLINOIS

SEE HISTORIC ILLINOIS

The fertile prairies in Illinois attracted the attention of French trader Louis Jolliet and Father Jacques Marquette as they explored the Mississippi and Illinois Rivers in 1673. France claimed this region until 1763 when she surrendered it to Great Britain by the Treaty of Paris. During the American Revolution George Rogers Clark and his small army scored a bloodless victory when they captured Kaskaskia for the Commonwealth of Virginia, and Illinois became a county of Virginia. This area was ceded to the United States in 1784, and became in turn a part of the Northwest Territory and the Indiana and Illinois territories. On December 3, 1818, Illinois entered the Union as the twenty-first state.

US 36 touches six counties which were a part of the Eighth Judicial Circuit. From 1839 to 1860 Abraham Lincoln followed the court as it moved from county seat to county seat within the circuit. Thus he came to such cities as Paris, Sullivan, Monticello, Decatur, and Springfield for the bi-annual terms.

West of Decatur this highway passes near the Lincoln Trail Homestead State Park on the banks of the Sangamon River. This was the site of the first Lincoln home in Illinois when the family came from Indiana in 1830. The following spring Thomas Lincoln moved to Coles County and Abraham moved on to New Salem, 20 miles northwest of Springfield. US 36 passes through Springfield where Lincoln's home and tomb are state memorials. Springfield is also the site of the Old State Capitol where Lincoln delivered his famous "House Divided" speech.

Lincoln, July 11, 1858.

Located: North side of US 36 just west of Indiana line.

OFFICIAL STATE MAP: H-10
EDGAR COUNTY

PONTIAC'S CONSPIRACY

On the site of Palermo, three miles east of here, according to tradition George Croghan, Deputy Superintendent of Indian Affairs, met the Ottawa Chief Pontiac in July, 1765, and made preliminary arrangements for the peace which ended the Indian uprising known as Pontiac's Conspiracy. Shortly afterward the treaty was concluded at Fort Ouiatenon (Lafayette, Indiana).

The Lewistown Trail, shown by a broken line, ran from Springfield to Galena via Lewistown.

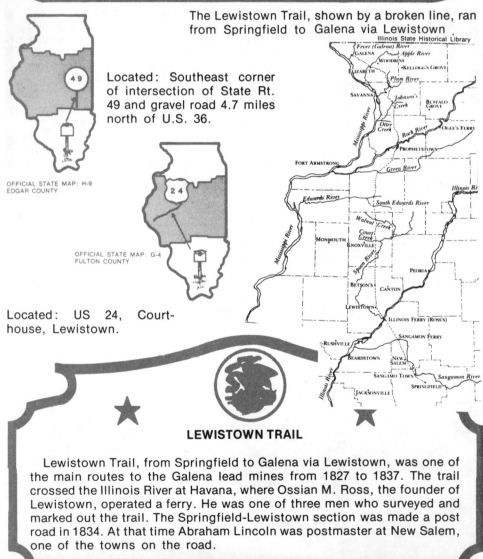

Illinois State Historical Library

Located: Southeast corner of intersection of State Rt. 49 and gravel road 4.7 miles north of U.S. 36.

OFFICIAL STATE MAP: H-9
EDGAR COUNTY

OFFICIAL STATE MAP: G-4
FULTON COUNTY

Located: US 24, Court-house, Lewistown.

LEWISTOWN TRAIL

Lewistown Trail, from Springfield to Galena via Lewistown, was one of the main routes to the Galena lead mines from 1827 to 1837. The trail crossed the Illinois River at Havana, where Ossian M. Ross, the founder of Lewistown, operated a ferry. He was one of three men who surveyed and marked out the trail. The Springfield-Lewistown section was made a post road in 1834. At that time Abraham Lincoln was postmaster at New Salem, one of the towns on the road.

116

CARTHAGE, ILLINOIS

Hancock County, established in 1829, had no permanent county seat for four years. On February 13, 1833, the General Assembly commissioned William Gilham, Scott Riggs, and John Hardin to establish a permanent county seat. The new settlement, located near the geographic center of the county, was named Carthage and was incorporated in 1837.

Joseph Smith, founder of the Mormon Church, and his brother Hyrum were shot to death in the Old Carthage Jail on June 27, 1844. Joseph had chosen Nauvoo as headquarters for the church in 1839, and by 1844 Hancock County was a Mormon center. However, unrest concerning the authority of the Mormon leaders was extensive. When an anti-Mormon newspaper in Nauvoo was destroyed, Joseph and Hyrum were jailed at Carthage to await trial. Governor Thomas Ford assigned the Carthage Grays, a militia unit, to guard them. A mob overpowered the guards and rushed the captives who with two Mormon friends, Willard Richards and John Taylor, occupied an unlocked, second-floor room in the jail.

Hyrum was killed, and the Prophet was shot several times before he fell from a window to the ground. Taylor, later the leader of the Church of Jesus Christ of Latter-day Saints (1877-1887), recovered from his wounds while Richards was uninjured. Conflict between the Mormons and their neighbors continued until the Mormons completed their exodus from Illinois (1846). The Mormons have restored the Old Carthage Jail.

During the 1858 U.S. senatorial campaign Stephen A. Douglas spoke at Carthage on October 11 and Abraham Lincoln spoke on October 22.

Located: Ill. 94, 2½ miles South of Carthage.

A representation of the death of Joseph Smith, founder of the Mormon Church, and his brother Hyrum, when they were killed at the Old Carthage Jail.

OFFICIAL STATE MAP G-2
HANCOCK COUNTY

Illinois State Historical Library

OFFICIAL STATE MAP F-1
HANCOCK COUNTY

Located: (1) Illinois 96, in turnout 3 miles east of Nauvoo. (2) Illinois 96, in rest area at west edge of Nauvoo.

Joseph and Hyrum Smith.

Illinois State Historical Library

NAUVOO, ILLINOIS

Nauvoo was once the site of a Sauk and Fox village. After the Indians moved west of the Mississippi, promoters attempted to develop town sites here but the marshy bottom lands attracted few settlers.

In 1839, the Mormon Prophet Joseph Smith chose the town, then called Commerce, as the home for his followers, who had been driven from Missouri. The Mormons named the community Nauvoo, said to mean "beautiful place," and obtained a special charter from the Illinois Legislature, which gave the city government its own courts, militia, university, and all other governmental powers not prohibited by the federal and state constitutions.

Mormon converts from all parts of America and Europe soon swelled the population to about 15,000, making Nauvoo one of the largest cities in Illinois by 1845. But some of the Mormons as well as their gentile neighbors began to resent the civil and religious authority of the Mormon leaders, and frictions in the area grew severe. When the Nauvoo City Council had an anti-Mormon newspaper destroyed, the Mormon leaders were arrested and jailed at Carthage. There, on June 27, 1844, an armed mob shot and killed Joseph Smith and his brother, Hyrum. Conflict between the Mormons and their neighbors continued until 1846 when the Mormons completed their exodus from the state.

In 1849, Etienne Cabet's followers, the Icarians, came to Nauvoo to practice their form of religious communism but dissensions soon weakened the colony. Their experiment lasted less than ten years.

Nauvoo from the Mississippi, looking down the river.

Located: Two markers on State Rt. 96, one near each city limit of Nauvoo.

HISTORIC NAUVOO

In 1839 the Mormons, or Latter Day Saints, settled at Nauvoo and made it their chief city. During their residence its population reached 15,000. After long friction with non-Mormons the Mormons were expelled in 1846. Three years later French communists called Icarians established a society here which lasted until 1857.

THE ICARIAN COMMUNITY IN NAUVOO

A communal society of French Icarians was established at Nauvoo in 1849. Led by Etienne Cabet, a French political theorist, the Icarians believed that all property must be held communally. The community was incorporated by the Illinois General Assembly in early 1851. At that time it had 335 members. They operated their own sawmill and grist mill and a commercial distillery. Disputes later arose over Cabet's leadership, and the Icarians began to resettle in other states. The Nauvoo community survived, however, until about 1860 -- longer than any other secular communal society in Illinois.

Located: Nauvoo Historical Museum, Nauvoo State Park.

Etienne Cabet.

Carthage, Illinois.

OFFICIAL STATE MAP: G-2
HANCOCK COUNTY

Located: On US 136 near western limits of Carthage.

THE "OLD JAIL"

In the Old Carthage Jail, which stands one block south of here, Joseph and Hyrum Smith, prophet and patriarch of the Mormon Church, were killed by a mob on June 27, 1844. Two years later the Mormons withdrew from Illinois, where they had settled in 1839, to the Great Salt Lake.

OFFICIAL STATE MAP: G-1
HANCOCK COUNTY

Located: US 136 at the
junction of Ill. 96 and U.S.
136 near Hamilton.

Map of the Mississippi River.

THY WONDROUS STORY, ILLINOIS

The fertile prairies in Illinois attracted the attention of French
trader Louis Jolliet and Father Jacques Marquette as they
explored the Mississippi and Illinois Rivers in 1673. France
claimed this region until 1763 when she surrendered it to Great
Britain by the Treaty of Paris. During the American Revolution
George Rogers Clark and his small army scored a bloodless
victory when they captured Kaskaskia for the Commonwealth of Virginia,
and Illinois became a county of Virginia. This area was ceded to the United
States in 1784, and became in turn a part of the Northwest Territory and
the Indiana territories. On December 3, 1818, Illinois entered the Union as
the twenty first state.

A short distance above Hamilton the lower rapids of the Mississippi
River obstructed steamboat navigation. In 1820 the steamboat **Western
Engineer** ascended to the foot of the rapids and three years later the
Virginia churned through the swift, shallow water. In the late 1830's
Lieutenant Robert E. Lee supervised drilling and blasting to widen and
deepen the river channel. When this project proved too costly and
ineffective an independent canal around the western side of the rapids was
started in 1866.

Between the Mississippi and Illinois Rivers Highway 136 cuts through
the Military Tract, an area used as bounty land for veterans of the War of
1812; north of Warsaw, site of Fort Edwards (1814); south of Nauvoo,
Morman city of the 1840's; and south of Dickson Mounds, ancient Indian
burial site near the Illinois River.

Stephen S. Phelps.

Located: Rest area on US 34, 2 miles east of the junction of US 34 and the Great River Road near Gulfport.

THY WONDROUS STORY, ILLINOIS

The fertile prairies in Illinois attracted the attention of French trader Louis Jolliet and Father Jacques Marquette as they explored the Mississippi Rivers in 1673. France claimed this region until 1763 when she surrendered it to Great Britain by the Treaty of Paris. During the American Revolution George Rogers Clark and his small army scored a bloodless victory when they captured Kaskaskia for the Commonwealth of Virginia, and Illinois became a county of Virginia. This area was ceded to the United States in 1784, and became in turn a part of the Northwest Territory and the Indiana and Illinois territories. On December 3, 1818, Illinois entered the Union as the twenty-first state.

During the Black Hawk War (1832) extensive hostilities in this region were avoided in part by the efforts of an Indian trader and merchant. Stephen Sumner Phelps, called Wah-wash-e-ne-qua (Hawkeye) by his Indian friends, established a trading post at Oquawka in 1828.

He helped convince Keokuk, an influential chief of the Sauk and Fox tribes, to remain out of the conflict. Otherwise western Illinois might have become a major battle ground. At another point, Phelps and his men defended the friendly aged Fox Chief Tama and his family against a group of irate soldiers thus averting an incident which could have extended the war into this area.

122

Butterfield Trail in Iroquois County.

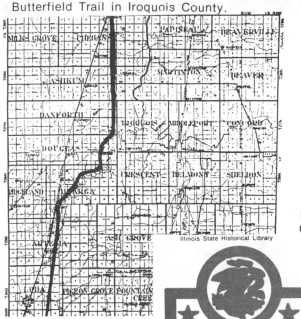

Illinois State Historical Library

OFFICIAL STATE MAP F-9
IROQUOIS COUNTY

Located: U.S. 24, east of Gilman.

BUTTERFIELD TRAIL

For many years Butterfield Trail was one of the main routes from east-central Illinois to the Chicago area. In 1831 Ben Butterfield marked out the trail from Danville to Lockport, where he had settled the previous year. The trail crossed Spring Creek two miles northwest of Buckley. Following an old Indian trail, it stayed west of the creek, continuing northward and passing this point. It avoided the Iroquois River and forded the Kankakee west of Bourbonnais. Thence it ran to Hickory Creek and the Des Plaines River. At a point near Joliet it forked, both forks leading to Chicago.

OFFICIAL STATE MAP: F-9
IROQUOIS COUNTY

Located: In Momence, on Ill. 1-17 North side of Ill. 1-17 just west of Bridge.

HUBBARD TRAIL

This trail was blazed by Gurdon S. Hubbard, 1822-1824, connecting the trading posts of the American Fur Company between Vincennes and Chicago. Momence, near the upper crossing of the Kankakee River, is on this trail. Known also as the Vincennes Trace, it is perpetuated today as State Highway No. 1.

The Lincoln Room of the Sandburg birthplace in Galesburg, Illinois.

THE CARL SANDBURG BIRTHPLACE

The Sandburg Birthplace, when constructed about 1870, was in an immigrant neighborhood inhabited mainly by railroad workers like August Sandburg, Carl Sandburg's father. The cottage provided only the rudiments of shelter for the Sandburgs. Rough vertical siding covered the exterior; the interior was unplastered and newspapers were pasted over the cracks to reduce drafts. The Sandburgs moved to successively larger homes during Carl's youth. After they moved from his birthplace in 1879, it was purchased by a carpenter who clapboarded the exterior, plastered the interior, and constructed the addition to the rear, leaving it much as it appears today.

Furnishings in the Sandburg Birthplace are simple and utilitarian; few amenities were found in homes of this type. Several pieces, including three living room chairs and the kitchen table, were used by the Sandburg family. Also original are the photographs of Clara and August Sandburg and the family Bible. Some of the furniture was made by craftsmen at the nearby Swedish settlement of Bishop Hill. The crowded bedroom with a trundle bed, the kitchen without running water, and the wood stove which provided the only heat in the house, all reflect typical living conditions for the working-class family of a century ago.

With the aid of a state appropriation in 1949, the addition to the rear of the Birthplace was rebuilt and furnished to serve as a museum of Sandburg's life and works. The Lincoln Room, as the addition was named, focuses on Sandburg's monumental Lincoln biography. Also on display are rare editions of Sandburg's first poetry, published in Galesburg; an autographed collection of Sandburg's books, which he had presented to his publisher, Alfred Harcourt; a typewriter which Sandburg used to write both **The Prairie Years** and **rootabaga stories**; and a portrait of Lincoln by N.C. Wyeth.

Carl Sandburg requested that he be buried beneath remembrance
rock in the park at the Sandburg birthplace.

Preservation of the Carl Sandburg Birthplace can be credited in large
part to the tireless efforts of a retired schoolteacher, Mrs. Adda George. It
was she who first identified the Birthplace, and when the property was put
up for sale in 1945, she formed the Carl Sandburg Birthplace Association
for the purpose of purchasing and restoring the structure. Later, the
Lincoln Room and park surrounding the Birthplace were added. On July 1,
1970, the Carl Sandburg Birthplace was deeded to the State of Illinois and
its operation was assumed by the Illinois State Historical Library and
Society.

Remembrance Rock is the title of Sandburg's only novel, and when a park
was proposed for the Birthplace, it was thought that a remembrance rock
would be an appropriate memorial to Sandburg. A suitable red granite
boulder was unearthed during the construction of Interstate 74, and after
being inscribed was placed in the park behind the Birthplace. Sandburg
was impressed by the park's Remembrance Rock, and asked that it be his
final resting place. The poet-historian's ashes were buried beneath the
rock in a special memorial service following his death in 1967.

Located: Sandburg Home,
Galesburg

OFFICIAL STATE MAP E-4
KNOX COUNTY

This photo of Carl Sandburg was taken on his
70th birthday in 1948 in doorway of his birthplace.

125

CARL SANDBURG BIRTHPLACE

Carl Sandburg, poet and historian, was born in this modest three-room cottage on January 6, 1878. He was the son of a Swedish immigrant railroad worker. Carl attended Lombard College in Galesburg, and his first poetry was published in this town. He later became a journalist and prolific author. His **Complete Poems** and a biography, **Abraham Lincoln: The War Years**, won Pulitzer prizes. He also wrote a novel, an autobiography, children's stories, and folksongs. After his death in 1967, his ashes were buried beneath Remembrance Rock behind his birthplace.

Located: Sandburg home, Galesburg

OFFICIAL STATE MAP: E-4
KNOX COUNTY

The Carl Sandburg birthplace in Galesburg, Illinois.

Located: South side Ill. 17 about 2 miles west of LaFayette.

OFFICIAL STATE MAP: E-4
KNOX COUNTY

FRAKER'S GROVE

In this area stood a Potawatomi village when Michael Fraker arrived from Kentucky about 1830. With Kindness and understanding he negotiated a peaceful settlement with the Indians and became the first permanent settler in northeastern Knox County. His grave is about one-half mile south of this point.

LINCOLN-DOUGLAS DEBATE

On October 7, 1858, Abraham Lincoln and Stephen A. Douglas met in Galesburg for the fifth of seven joint debates. From a platform erected along the east side of Old Main on the Knox College campus Lincoln said: "He is blowing out the moral lights around us, when he contends that whoever wants slaves has a right to hold them."

The Lincoln Douglas Debate at Galesburg.
Illinois State Historical Library

Located: U.S. 34 NE (200' from city limits) Galesburg.

OFFICIAL STATE MAP: E-4
KNOX COUNTY

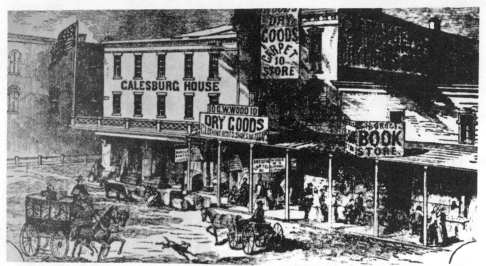

Galesburg, Illinois.

OFFICIAL STATE MAP: E-4
KNOX COUNTY

Located: In a turnout on the north side of US 150, 10 miles southeast of Galesburg.

GALESBURG, ILLINOIS

In 1834, George Washington Gale, Presbyterian minister of Whitesboro, New York, evolved a plan to form a community and manual labor college in the Midwest to train missionaries. His original plan was to purchase a township of government land at $1.25 an acre, sell it at $5 an acre, and apply the profits to an endowment for the college. Three sections of land were to be reserved for the college and community. In 1835, a committee of his followers picked the site. In the next two years settlers established Log City, a temporary town, and built Galesburg nearby. It was incorporated in 1841 and obtained the county seat from Knoxville in 1873.

Knox College, chartered in 1837, began holding classes in 1838. Knox was strongly influenced by its religious origins but it gradually broadened its educational objectives. In 1930 Knox absorbed Lombard College founded by the Universalists in 1851 as Illinois Liberal Institute.

Galesburg was a center of temperance and anti-slavery movements for many years and it was an important station on the Underground Railroad before the Civil War. On October 7, 1858, the fifth Lincoln-Douglas debate was held on Knox Campus at "Old Main" which was named a National Historic Landmark in 1936. Galesburg is the birthplace of Carl Sandburg, noted poet and Lincoln biographer. His parents were part of a large influx of Swedish immigrants who settled in Galesburg in the 1850's.

Located: On US 24 about 2½ miles east of Chatsworth.

THE CHATSWORTH WRECK
MIDNIGHT, AUGUST 10-11, 1887

One half mile north on the Toledo, Peoria & Western Railroad occurred one of the worst wrecks in American rail history. An excursion train--two engines and approximately twenty wooden coaches from Peoria to Niagara Falls, struck a burning culvert. Of the 500 passengers about 85 perished and scores were injured.

Chatsworth wreck.

This is the original announcement of the arrival of Lincoln's funeral train in Lincoln, Illinois.

OFFICIAL STATE MAP: G-6
LOGAN COUNTY

Located: Lincoln, Illinois, Broadway & Sangamon, NW side of GM & O tracks.

ABRAHAM LINCOLN AND LINCOLN, ILLINOIS

Near this site Abraham Lincoln christened the town with the juice of a watermelon when the first lots were sold on August 27, 1853. President-elect Lincoln spoke here, November 21, 1860, while traveling to Chicago and Lincoln's funeral train stopped here, May 3, 1865, before completing the trip to Springfield.

Located: East side of US 66
in rest area on the northwest
edge of Elkhart.

Illinois State Historical Library

John the Baptist Chapel, Elkhart Cemetery,
Elkhart, Illinois.

ELKHART, ILLINOIS

Elkhart city in Logan County is typical of the many Illinois villages whose growth was spurred by the arrival of the railroad. Founded by John Shockey in 1855, two years after the coming of the Alton and Sangamon Railroad, now the Gulf Mobile and Ohio, Elkhart was for many years one of the largest shipping points on this line.

Southeast of this site, on Elkhart Hill, is the mansion "oglehurst," home and burial place of Richard J. Oglesby (1824-1899), three times elected governor of the state of Illinois (1864, 1872, 1884). Ten days following his second inauguration he was elected United States Senator by the Illinois Legislature and served in that capacity until 1879. Governor Oglesby moved to Elkhart in 1890, following his retirement from public life.

Another prominent Elkhart resident was John Dean Gillett (1819-1883), one of the cattle kings of the prairies. A New Englander by birth, he came to Logan County in 1838. Through his skill in the raising and feeding of cattle, his name became a byword for superior quality beef in both this country and in England. At the time of his death, Gillett's land holdings totaled more than 16,000 acres.

Captain Adam H. Bogardus (1833-1913), wildfowl market hunter, conservationist and champion wingshot, made his home for many years in Elkhart. In 1878, he defeated Aubrey Coventry, English champion wingshot, 79 to 78. Returning to the United States, Bogardus toured with William "Buffalo Bill" Cody's "The Wild West."

DESKINS TAVERN

On this site Dr. John Deskins erected a tavern in 1836. Abraham Lincoln, David Davis and other lawyers frequently stayed overnight here while the Eighth Judicial Circuit Court was in session at the Postville court house. The judge, lawyers, litigants, witnesses, jurors and prisoners often shared the same dining table.

Lincoln College

Illinois State Historical Library

Located: Lincoln, Illinois, 5th & Madison.

OFFICIAL STATE MAP: G-6
LOGAN COUNTY

Located: Lincoln, Illinois, 300 Keokuk St..

LINCOLN COLLEGE

On Abraham Lincoln's last birthday, February 12, 1865, ground was broken for Lincoln University, now Lincoln College. The town proprietors, Robert B. Latham, John D. Gillett and Virgil Hickox, donated the tract of land for the original campus, and named the school in honor of their friend, Abraham Lincoln.

Located: Lincoln, Illinois, 501 Broadway.

Lincoln House, Lincoln, Illinois.

THE LINCOLN HOUSE

On this site the town proprietors erected the original Lincoln House in 1854. Leonard Volk met Abraham Lincoln on the sidewalk in front of the hotel on July 16, 1858, and arranged to make Lincoln's life mask later.

LOGAN COUNTY CIRCUIT COURT

On this site stood two former Logan County courthouses in which Abraham Lincoln practiced law from 1856 until elected president. During the March term, 1859, Lincoln substituted for David Davis as the presiding judge of the Logan County Circuit Court.

Logan County Courthouse, Lincoln, Illinois

Located: Lincoln, Illinois, Courthouse.

133

Located: On north side of old court house, one block from 121.

The Mt. Pulaski Courthouse.   Illinois State Historical Library

MOUNT PULASKI COURT HOUSE

Mount Pulaski was the seat of Logan County from 1848 to 1854. In this building, then the court house, Abraham Lincoln attended court twice a year.

This is the Postville Courthouse where Abraham Lincoln, as a member of the traveling bar of the Eighth Judicial Circuit, attended court twice a year.   Illinois State Historical Library

Located: On north side of street, U.S. 66, Lincoln, Illinois.

POSTVILLE COURT HOUSE SITE

From 1839 to 1848 the seat of Logan County was Postville, which centered in the court house located on this site. In this structure Abraham Lincoln, a member of the traveling bar of the Eighth Judicial Circuit, attended court twice a year.

POSTVILLE PARK

In 1835 Russell Post, a Baltimore adventurer, laid out the town of Postville which became the first Logan County seat. The town square is now Postville Park. Here Abraham Lincoln and his friends played townball (a predecessor of baseball), threw the maul (a heavy wooden hammer), and pitched horseshoes.

Located: Lincoln, Illinois, 5th & Washington Sts..

OFFICIAL STATE MAP: G-6
LOGAN COUNTY

ROBERT B. LATHAM HOME

On this site stood the home of Robert B. Latham who joined John D. Gillett and Virgil Hickox to found the town of Lincoln in 1853. Abraham Lincoln, judges and lawyers of the Eighth Judicial Circuit were frequent guests at his home.

OFFICIAL STATE MAP: G-6
LOGAN COUNTY

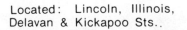

Located: Lincoln, Illinois, Delavan & Kickapoo Sts..

Latham home, Lincoln, Illinois.

Illinois State Historical Library

135

OFFICIAL STATE MAP: G-6
LOGAN COUNTY

Stephen Arnold Douglas

Located: Lincoln, Illinois,
Decatur & Sangamon Sts..

STEPHEN A. DOUGLAS SPEECH

On this site during the senatorial campaign of 1858 Stephen A. Douglas spoke to a Democratic political rally in a circus tent on September 4th. Douglas' opponent for the Senate seat, Abraham Lincoln, was on the train from Bloomington to Springfield and stopped to hear the speech.

136

LINCOLN NATIONAL MEMORIAL HIGHWAY

From the site of the Lincoln cabin on the Sangamon River three miles south of here to the Wabash River opposite Vincennes, the Lincoln National Memorial Highway follows substantially the route taken by the Lincoln family in their migration from Indiana to Illinois in the spring of 1800.

Located: South side of US 36 in turnout at spur to Lincoln Homestead State Park.

OFFICIAL STATE MAP: H-6
MACON COUNTY

This map shows the route travelled by the Thomas Lincoln family in coming from Indiana to Illinois in the year 1830.

Abraham Lincoln Memorial Highway Association.

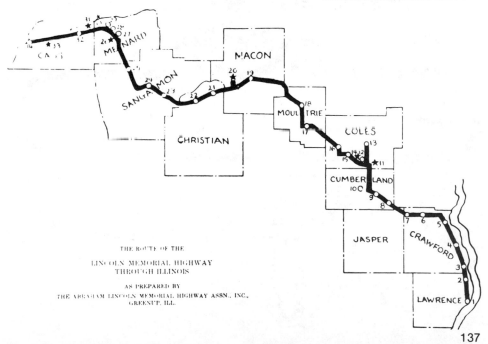

THE ROUTE OF THE

LINCOLN MEMORIAL HIGHWAY
THROUGH ILLINOIS

AS PREPARED BY

THE ABRAHAM LINCOLN MEMORIAL HIGHWAY ASSN., INC.,
GREENUP, ILL.

Lincoln Home, Macon County, Illinois.

Located: on US 36 west of Decatur on South side of US 36 in turnout at spur to Lincoln Homestead State Park.

LINCOLN'S FIRST ILLINOIS HOME

On an eminence overlooking the Sangamon River three miles south of here stood the first home of Lincoln in Illinois. To this site came the Lincoln family in March, 1830. Here they lived until 1831, when the parents removed to Coles County and Abraham set out on his own career.

SITE OF THE LINCOLN CABIN

The Lincoln cabin stood near the north bank of the Sangamon River about 600 yards to the east.

Located: Lincoln Trail Homestead State Park.

138

BLOOMINGTON-NORMAL, ILLINOIS

The first settlement in this area in 1822 was called Keg Grove. By the time a post office was established in 1829 the settlement was known as Blooming Grove. McLean County was organized the following year and Bloomington, which was laid out in 1831 just north of Blooming Grove on 22½ acres of land donated by James Allin, was selected as county seat. It was incorporated as a town in 1843 and a city in 1850. In 1853 Illinois Wesleyan University was chartered here and in 1857 Normal University, first state-supported school of higher education in Illinois, was established in North Bloomington which soon changed its name to Normal.

The state Republican Party was formally organized in Bloomington in 1856 at a convention called to protest the Kansas-Nebraska Bill, which made possible the westward extension of slavery. It was at this convention that Abraham Lincoln delivered his "Lost Speech", so called because no record of it was kept. Several of Lincoln's close associates were local residents, including Jesse Fell, credited with the founding of Normal, Leonard Swett, lawyer and campaigner for Lincoln, and David Davis, appointed to the United States Supreme Court by Lincoln (1862-1877) and later United States senator.

Other distinguished residents include governors John M. Hamilton and Joseph Fifer; Adlai Stevenson I, Vice-President under Cleveland; and Adlai Stevenson II, governor, twice presidential candidate, and United Nations Ambassador. The David Davis mansion is located at Monroe Drive and Davis Street and is open to the public.

Located: (1) In a turnout on the north side of Illinois 9, just west of Bloomington. (2) In a turnout on the northeast side of Illinois 150 about 3 miles northwest of Bloomington.

OFFICIAL STATE MAP: G-7
MCLEAN COUNTY

OFFICIAL STATE MAP: G-7
MCLEAN COUNTY

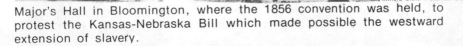

Illinois State Historical Library

Major's Hall in Bloomington, where the 1856 convention was held, to protest the Kansas-Nebraska Bill which made possible the westward extension of slavery.

139

The portrait of Judge Davis hangs above the fireplace in the living room of Clover Lawn.

Historic Site

OFFICIAL STATE MAP: G-7
MCLEAN COUNTY

Located: Davis and Monroe Streets, Bloomington.

CLOVER LAWN--THE DAVID DAVIS MANSION

The land on which the Davis Mansion now stands was originally part of a two-hundred acre farm owned by Jesse Fell, the founder of Normal and the lawyer who sold his Bloomington practice to Davis. Fell lost heavily on land investments following the Panic of 1837, and in 1844 turned the farm over to Davis in exchange for his home in town and the settlement of an outstanding loan. Davis soon added another thousand acres to the farm, enlarged the two-story frame house, and named the estate "Clover Lawn." Abraham Lincoln was an overnight guest there before delivering his famous "Lost Speech" at the 1856 state Republican convention in Bloomington.

After he was named to the Supreme Court, Judge Davis considered moving to Washington, but respected his wife's wish to remain in Bloomington and realized that building on this site would enhance the value of his nearby property. He selected one of the Midwest's most prominent architects, Alfred H. Piquenard, to design his new home.

The mansion which Piquenard designed is a variation of the Italian villa style, which admirably fitted the Davis' needs. According to the noted architect A.J. Downing, "The Italian style is one that expresses not wholly the country life, nor the town life, but....a mingling of both." The Davis home was one of the most imposing in the Midwest when built. It covers an area 64 by 88 feet, has a three-story tower with a mansard roof, and contains twenty rooms plus a full basement and attic. The home has verandas, bay windows, bracketed eaves, and ornamental cast iron railings, all typical of the Victorian period.

Construction on the mansion began in May, 1870, when the old Fell house was moved to one side. Only the finest materials were used. The yellow hard-burned face brick came from the noted kilns of Milwaukee and the foundation sandstone from Ohio. The window frames and quoining are of limestone. The ornamental ironwork was supplied by firms in

This photo shows the living room of the Davis Mansion.

Philadelphia and St. Louis. Some materials had to be imported. The vestibule floor is English tile, the plate glass is French, and the eight fireplace mantles are of Italian marble.

By the fall of 1870, the rough walls were up and the roof was completed by the following spring. Work then began on the interior. By the end of 1871, the mantles, doors, gas lighting fixtures, and furnace were installed. Among the last details were putting up the interior shutters and applying the frescoing, as the elaborate stencil painting of the walls and ceilings was then termed. During the summer of 1872, Mrs. Davis selected the furniture, carpets, and draperies at Alexander T. Stuart & Co. and other fine New York stores. By early autumn, the carpets were down and the Davis family settled into the home which had taken more than two years to complete and cost more than $50,000.

Late Victorian furniture in the dining room of Davis mansion — note the stenciled ceiling.

By the time the Mansion was built, Clover Lawn had become an urban estate bounded by Locust Street, Colton Avenue, Jefferson Street, and the Illinois Central Railroad; and Judge Davis was subdividing adjacent properties into building lots. The grounds reflect the urban environment. A formal oval drive surrounds the mansion, and the trees which flanked the approach drive still stretch southward to Jefferson Street. To the east of the mansion is a small but elegant formal garden. To the rear, an elaborate brick wood house designed by Piquenard complements the mansion. The original wooden carriage house, barn, and stable remain, although the garage is a twentheth-century addition. The family traditionally maintained three teams of horses, three or four saddle horses, a pony for the children, two cows, and assorted pigs and chickens.

Clover Lawn was reduced to its present size in 1959 and was donated to the State of Illinois by the DAvis heirs the following year. It had been the home of four successive generations of the Davis family, and stands preserved today as an example of the gracious living of a bygone age.

OFFICIAL STATE MAP: G-7
MCLEAN COUNTY

Located: 100 East Monroe, Bloomington.

Illinois State Historical Library

Clover Lawn — the David Davis mansion.

DAVID DAVIS MANSION

This Victorian mansion was the home of Judge David Davis, an associate of Abraham Lincoln's. Construction began in 1870 and was completed in 1872. The house is built of yellow hard-burned face brick with stone quoins in the corners. It is 64 feet wide, extends 88 feet back, and has a tower that rises 50 feet above the ground. The lavish interior includes eight marble fireplaces. Davis was appointed by President Lincoln to the Supreme Court of the United States in 1862 and became a United States senator in 1877. He returned to Illinois in 1883 and lived here again until his death in 1886.

142

HOME OF ADLAI E. STEVENSON I

This was the home of Adlai E. Stevenson I, vice-president of the United States, 1893-1897. Stevenson was born in Kentucky in 1835 and came to Bloomington in 1852. He attended Illinois Wesleyan University in Bloomington and Centre College in Kentucky. He began to practice law in Metamora, Illinois, in 1858 and returned to Bloomington in 1868. A lifelong Democrat, Stevenson was elected to Congress in 1874 and 1878. He served as First Assistant Postmaster General in President Grover Cleveland's first administration, 1893-1897. Stevenson bought this house in 1889. He died in 1914.

Located: 901 N. McLean, Bloomington ·

OFFICIAL STATE MAP: G-7
MCLEAN COUNTY

This is the home of Adlai E. Stevenson I, vice-president of the United States from 1893-1897.

Illinois State Historical Library

Illinois State Historical Library

Joseph W. Fifer, governor of Illinois from 1889-1893.

Located: 909 N. McLean, Bloomington.

HOME OF JOSEPH W. FIFER

This was the home of Joseph W. Fifer, Republican Governor of Illinois, 1889-1893. Fifer was born in Virginia in 1840 and came to Illinois in 1857. During the Civil War he served in the 33rd Illinois Infantry Regiment. He graduated from Illinois Wesleyan in Bloomington in 1868 and began to practice law the next year. After being corporation counsel of Bloomington for one year and state's attorney of McLean County for eight years, he served two terms as state senator. He moved to these premises in 1893, at the end of his term as governor, and lived in this red brick house from its completion in 1896 to his death in 1938.

Located: Ill. 97, at entrance to Rosehill Cemetery (Ill. 123) one mile east of Petersburg.

DR. BENJAMIN FRANKLIN STEPHENSON, 1823-1871

Founder of the Grand Army of the Republic, Menard County resident, Rush Medical College graduate 1850, surgeon 14th Illinois Volunteers 1861-1864, he originated the G.A.R. name, ritual, constitution of Post No. 1, Decatur, April 6, 1866, called first national G.A.R. convention and was its first adjutant general.

LINCOLN'S STORE PARTNER

William F. Berry, 1811-1835, is buried two miles west in the cemetery of Rock Creek Cumberland Presbyterian Church. His father, the Rev. John M. Berry, founded the church in 1822.

Abraham Lincoln and Berry were partners in a store at New Salem in 1832-1833. Berry was a corporal in Captain Abraham Lincoln's Company in the Black Hawk War.

Located: On Ill. Highway 97 two miles east of Rock Creek Cemetery West side of 97.

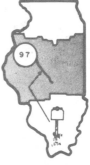

OFFICIAL STATE MAP: H-5
MENARD COUNTY

The interior of the Lincoln-Berry store in New Salem.

Illinois State Historical Library

145

State
Park

OFFICIAL STATE MAP H-5
MENARD COUNTY

Located: New
Salem.

Illinois State Historical Library

This painting of New Salem on the east mall, south corridor, of
the Capitol Building.

LINCOLN'S NEW SALEM STATE PARK

Lincoln's New Salem State Park is the village where Abraham Lincoln
spent his early adulthood. The six years Lincoln spent in New Salem
formed a turning point in his career. From the gangling youngster who
came to the village in 1831 with no definite objectives, he became a man of
purpose as he embarked upon a career of law and statesmanship. It was
from New Salem that he was first elected to the Illinois General Assembly
in 1834. He departed from New Salem for residence in Springfield in 1837.

Lincoln was engaged in a variety of activities while he was at New
Salem. He clerked in a store, chopped wood, enlisted in the Black Hawk
War, served as postmaster and deputy surveyor, failed in business and
was elected to the Illinois General Assembly in 1834 after an unsuccessful
try in 1832.

Strangely, the six years that Lincoln spent in New Salem almost
completely encompass the town's brief history. The community was
growing and thriving when Lincoln reached there in 1831, but in 1839, just
two years after he left New Salem for Springfield to practice law, the
county seat was established at nearby Petersburg. Thereafter, New Salem
declined rapidly.

The first active step toward re-creating New Salem came in 1906 when
William Randolph Hearst, lecturing at the Old Salem Chautauqua near
Petersburg, became interested in the preservation of the site, bought it
and transferred it in trust to the Chautauqua Association. In 1917, the Old
Salem Lincoln League was formed in Petersburg to carry on research and

146

keep alive interest in New Salem. In 1918, with the consent of Mr. Hearst, the land was transferred to the State of Illinois, and the following year became a state park.

During the years that followed public interest in the park grew steadily and visitors from all over the nation came in increasing numbers. In 1931, the General Assembly appropriated $50,000 for permanent improvements to the park, and the cabin construction was begun. The cornerstone for the first of the reconstructed buildings, the Berry-Lincoln Store, was laid November 17, 1932.

The only original building in the park is the Onstot Cooper Shop. It was built in 1835, moved to Petersburg in 1840 and returned to New Salem in 1922 by the Old Salem Chautauqua League. It was in this shop that Lincoln studied by the light of a fire made from Cooper's shavings.

Twelve timber houses, the Rutledge Tavern, ten shops, stores, industries and a school where church services were held, have been reproduced and furnished as they were in the 1830's. The furnishings, including many articles actually used by the New Salem people of Lincoln's time and others dating back to the same period, were assembled and donated to the state by the Old Salem Chautauqua League. The collection includes such authentic early nineteenth century articles as wheat cradles, candle molds, cord beds, flax shuttles, wool cards, dough and cornmeal chests and early American pewter and earthenware. For the doctors' offices there are mortars and pestles, surgeons' instruments, medicine chests and old medical texts; for the cobbler's shop, awls, lasts and rasps; for the tavern, old kitchen furnishings, utensils and tablewares; and for the stores, calico bolts, implements, jars and items of merchandise typical of the times.

Flower and vegetable gardens and trees have been planted for historical authenticity and to re-create the original village scene. Red haw, Osage orange hedges, wild crab, wild plum, witch hazel, wild blackberry, wild gooseberry, and other trees and plants popular with New Salem pioneers have been planted. At the homes of two doctors in the village, herb gardens grow again.

The Denton Offutt Store in New Salem, Illinois.

Illinois State Historical Library

147

Rogers Post Office and Store. Site of "Long Nine" banquet.

Located: Long Nine Museum, Athens.

OFFICIAL STATE MAP: H-5
MENARD COUNTY

29

★ "LONG NINE" BANQUET SITE ★

In this structure, built about 1832, residents of the Athens area held a banquet on August 3, 1837, for the "Long Nine"--Abraham Lincoln and the other state legislators from Sangamon County. The men, whose height totaled fifty-four feet, were honored for their success in the Tenth General Assembly in changing the state capital from Vandalia to Springfield. State offices were moved in 1839. At the Athens banquet Lincoln gave a toast: "Sangamon County will ever be true to her best interests and never more so than in reciprocating the good feelings of the citizens of Athens and neighborhood."

MENTOR GRAHAM
1800-1886
TEACHER OF ABRAHAM LINCOLN

"I think I may say that he was my scholar and I was his teacher." At New Salem Lincoln read Graham's books and in 1833 studied grammar and surveying. Teacher in Kentucky and Illinois more than fifty years, Graham died in South Dakota. In 1933 his remains were removed here.

OFFICIAL STATE MAP: H-5
MENARD COUNTY

Abraham Lincoln's teacher, Mentor Graham and wife, from a tintype.

Located: In Farmers Point Cemetery, two miles south of New Salem.

G. V. Black.

Located: 300 East State, Jacksonville.

GREENE VARDIMAN BLACK

G.V. Black, "Father of Modern Dentistry," was born in 1836 on a farm near Winchester, Illinois. He studied medicine and dentistry and in 1857 began his practice of dentistry in Winchester. After serving in the Civil War, he resumed his dental practice in Jacksonville. His home and last office stood on this site. Here he did extensive research, wrote hundreds of papers and books, and invented many dental instruments. Many of his ideas on care and restoration of teeth became the accepted methods. Dr. Black taught dental pathology at several dental schools. He moved to Chicago in 1897 to become dean of the Northwestern University Dental School, serving until his death in 1915.

JACKSONVILLE, ILLINOIS

Jacksonville, county seat of Morgan County, was founded in 1825 and named for Andrew Jackson. It was a contender for the state capital in 1837.

Jacksonville was an early education center. Seven men known as the "Yale Band" were instrumental in founding Illinois College, one of the earliest colleges chartered in Illinois, in 1829. It graduated the first college class in Illinois in 1835. Jonathan Baldwin Turner, outstanding faculty member and leader in agricultural education, settled here in 1833. For many years he led the fight for land grant colleges resulting in the Morrill Act (1862). The Jacksonville Female Academy was the first women's school incorporated by the Illinois Legislature (1835). In 1846 the Illinois Methodist Conference established the Illinois Conference Female Academy which became MacMurray College (1930). The Illinois School for the Deaf and the Illinois Braille and Sight Saving School are also here. Dr. Greene Vardiman Black, internationally recognized pioneer in modern dentistry, opened an office here in 1863 and practiced until 1897.

Jacksonville was the home of three Illinois governors--Joseph Duncan (1834-1838), Richard Yates (1861-1865), and Richard Yates, Jr. (1901-1905). Stephen A. Douglas and William Jennings Bryan began their law practices here in 1834 and 1883 respectively. Douglas was Morgan County prosecuting attorney; Illinois legislator, Secretary of State, and Supreme Court Judge; U.S. representative and senator; and presidential candidate against Abraham Lincoln in 1860. Bryan, an Illinois College graduate, was a U.S. representative, U.S. Secretary of State, and three times presidential candidate.

Located: 1) U.S. 67, north of Jacksonville. 2) U.S. 36-54, east of Jacksonville; 3) U.S. 36-54, west of Jacksonville.

OFFICIAL STATE MAP I-4
MORGAN COUNTY

OFFICIAL STATE MAP: I-4
MORGAN COUNTY

Illinois State Historical Library

The home of Richard Yates, governor of Illinois, from 1861-1865.

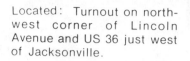

Located: Turnout on northwest corner of Lincoln Avenue and US 36 just west of Jacksonville.

ILLINOIS COLLEGE

Founded in 1829 by Presbyterian and Congregational ministers, it was the first college in Illinois to graduate a class. The first graduate was Richard Yates, Civil War governor. Alma mater of William Jennings Bryan, '81. Beecher Hall, the state's oldest college building, is on the campus one-half mile north.

Beecher Hall on the campus of Illinois College is the oldest college building in Illinois.

Illinois State Historical Library

JUBILEE COLLEGE

Jubilee College, two miles to the north, was established by Philander Chase, first Protestant Episcopal Bishop of Illinois, as one of the state's early institutions of higher learning. First students were received in 1840, and the school continued to operate until 1868. Jubilee College is now a state park.

Located: On north side of US 150 at intersection of gravel road leading to Jubilee (second gravel road west of Kickapoo).

OFFICIAL STATE MAP F-5
PEORIA COUNTY

Early day Jubilee College.
Illinois State Historical Library

Fort Crevecoeur.

Located: Grand View Park, III. 29, Peoria, Illinois. West side, 2.5 mile north of US 150.

PIMITEOUI

Meaning "Fat Lake," Illinois Indian name for Peoria Lake. Here passed Jolliet and Marquette in 1673. Established near the lake were Ft. Crevecoeur, 1680; Ft. St. Louis, 1691-92; Old Peoria Fort and Village, 1730; Peorias, 1778; Ft. Clark, 1813; French Trading House "Opa Post," before 1818. Americans settled on the site of the city of Peoria in 1819.

ZION PROTESTANT EPISCOPAL CHURCH

Founded by the Rt. Rev. Philander Chase, first bishop of Illinois, 1845. Restored and rededicated by the Rt. Rev. William L. Essex, Bishop of Quincy, November 4, 1945.

Located: Brimfield, Illinois, on side of building, 1 block south of US 150 and two blocks west of curve at E. edge of Brimfield.

Rev. Philander Chase.

PEORIA, ILLINOIS

The city of Peoria, hub of one of the largest industrial areas in the state, lies in the heart of the fertile and rolling terrain of the Illinois River Valley. Peoria was named for the Indian tribe that once lived here.

In 1673 Pere Jacques Marquette and the explorer Louis Jolliet passed northward through Lake Peoria, the wide portion of the Illinois River on which the city is located. Robert Cavelier, Sieur de LaSalle, with Henri de Tonti built Fort Crevecoeur on the bluffs opposite the present city in 1680. The fort was abandoned the same year. Eleven years later Tonti returned. He and Francois de LaForest then built Fort St. Louis near the narrows of the river.

In 1813 Illinois and Missouri Militia units built Fort Clark in the area of present downtown Peoria. In 1825 Peoria was named the seat of the newly created Peoria County. Peoria was surveyed and laid out in 1826 by William S. Hamilton, son of Alexander Hamilton. It was incorporated as a town in 1837 and as a city in 1845.

At the courthouse square on October 16, 1854, Abraham Lincoln delivered one of his first speeches that publicly denounced slavery. It was a reply to a speech made by Stephen A. Douglas in support of the Kansas-Nebraska Act.

The city's industry is both wide and varied. For many years Peoria has been known for its production of tractors, farm implements, and distilled liquors.

Bradley Polytechnic Institute (now Bradley University), located near the west edge of the city, was founded in 1897 with gifts from Lydia Bradley.

Located: Detweiler Park, Peoria.

OFFICIAL STATE MAP F-5
PEORIA COUNTY

Americans settled on the site of the city of Peoria in 1819. This picture depicts Peoria in about 1846.

Illinois State Historical Library

OFFICIAL STATE MAP: I-2
PIKE COUNTY

Located: US 36, 1 mile east of the Missouri state line near East Hannibal.

THY WONDROUS STORY, ILLINOIS

The fertile prairies in Illinois attracted the attention of French trader Louis Jolliet and Father Jacques Marquette as they explored the Mississippi and Illinois Rivers in 1673. France claimed this region until 1763 when she surrendered it to Great Britain by the Treaty of Paris. During the American Revolution George Rogers Clark and his small army scored a bloodless victory when they captured Kaskaskia for the Commonwealth of Virginia, and Illinois became a county of Virginia. This area was ceded to the United States in 1784, and became in turn a part of the Northwest Territory and the Indiana and Illinois territories. On December 3, 1818, Illinois entered the Union as the twenty-first state.

The highway markers which designate U.S. 54 in Illinois as the 33rd Division Memorial Highway were dedicated on Memorial Day, 1963. The 33rd Division was organized in August, 1917 from National Guard units of the state of Illinois. It became famous in the Meuse-Argonne offensive and by November 11, 1918 was poised for a smashing break through the Hindenburg line. In World War II the division fought in the Pacific area and liberated Baguio, the summer capital of the Philippines.

U.S. 54 passes through Pittsfield where John Nicolay and John Hay, President Abraham Lincoln's private secretaries, formed their friendship. Stephen A. Douglas studied law and taught in Winchester and held his first elective office in Jacksonville. Lincoln's home, tomb and the Old State Capitol are in Springfield and a courthouse where Lincoln practiced is in Mt. Pulaski.

This mural, "River Boat and Bridge" was painted for the Pittsfield Post Office by William S. Schwartz in 1938.

Illinois State Historical Library

Illinois State Historical Library

U.S. 36 passes through Winchester where Stephen A. Douglas studied and taught law.

OFFICIAL STATE MAP I-2
PIKE COUNTY

Location: Southeast side of US 54, 2.3 miles east of the Mississippi River B r i d g e near Louisiana, Missouri.

THY WONDROUS STORY, ILLINOIS

The fertile prairies in Illinois attracted the attention of French trader Louis Jolliet and Father Jacques Marquette as they explored the Mississippi and Illinois Rivers in 1673. France claimed this region until 1763 when she surrendered it to Great Britain by the Treaty of Paris. During the American Revolution George Rogers Clark and his small army scored a bloodless victory when they captured Kaskaskia for the Commonwealth of Virginia, and Illinois became a county of Virginia. This area was ceded to the United States in 1784, and became in turn a part of the Northwest Terriroty and the Indiana and Illinois territories. On December 3, 1818, Illinois entered the union as the twenty-first state.

U.S. 36 passes through the center of the land of Lincoln with its many historic sites. In the picturesque city of Pittsfield in this county John Nicolay and John Hay, President Lincoln's private secretaries, formed their friendship. Farther along this highway Stephen A. Douglas, Lincoln's opponent for the Senate in 1858 and the Presidency in 1860, studied law and taught in Winchester and held his first elective office in Jacksonville.

The Springfield area has a series of state memorials related to Lincoln. New Salem, carefully recreated as the village where Lincoln lived, is northwest of the city and his home, tomb and the Old State Capitol are in the present state capital. West of Decatur is a state park on the site of Lincoln's first home in Illinois.

ABRAHAM LINCOLN

Abraham Lincoln was born in Hardin County, Kentucky, February 12, 1809. He moved with his family to Indiana in 1816 and to Illinois in 1830. His first home in Illinois was eight miles southwest of Decatur. In 1831 he moved alone to New Salem, twenty miles northwest of Springfield, and there he operated a general store and served as postmaster and deputy county surveyor. He served as a representative in the state legislature, 1834-1842, and in 1837 was a leader in the effort to move the state government from Vandalia to Springfield. Springfield became the capital in 1839.

In 1836 Lincoln was admitted to the bar, and in 1837 he moved to Springfield and began his law practice. He argued cases in a number of circuit courts, especially those in counties in the Eighth Judicial Circuit. He spent much of his public life at the Old State Capitol in downtown Springfield. In 1842 he married Mary Todd and in 1844 purchased his home at Eighth and Jackson Streets in Springfield. As a Whig, Lincoln was elected a representative to the United States Congress in 1846. As a Republican he opposed Stephen A. Douglas for the United States Senate in 1858, and the debates between the candidates made Lincoln nationally prominent though Douglas won the race.

Lincoln was elected President of the United States in 1860, and the election of a Republican prompted the southern states to secede from the Union. Lincoln was inaugurated March 4, 1861, and the Civil War began April 12. The original war aim of the North was restoration of the Union; after 1862, freeing the slaves became another objective. Lincoln was reelected in 1864. At his second inauguration in 1865 he pled for a conciliatory attitude toward the South. He pursued the war to a successful conclusion, capped by Lee's surrender to Grant on April 9, 1865. Five days later Lincoln was assassinated in Ford's Theatre in Washington. He is buried in Oak Ridge Cemetery, Springfield.

This is the earliest known photograph of Abraham Lincoln.   Illinois State Historical Library

Located: Southbound Lanes, I-55, northeast of Springfield, N. of Sangamon River.

OFFICIAL STATE MAP: H-5
SANGAMON COUNTY

The Talisman.

Located: Rest Area on east side of north bound lane on Interstate 55 just south of the Sangamon River.

ABRAHAM LINCOLN AND THE TALISMAN

Prior to the coming of the railroads, Springfield was handicapped by inadequate transportation facilities. Early in 1832, Vincent A. Bogue, Springfield businessman and promoter, planned to supply the Sangamon River region with steamboat service. He chartered the **Talisman**, a 150-ton upper cabin steamer 136 feet long with a 48 foot beam, and obtained cargo in Cincinnati. On February 5 the journey began down the Ohio River up the Mississippi to St. Louis, on to the Illinois, up to Beardstown, and via the Sangamon to the Springfield area.

Springfield citizens were enthusiastic and had raised funds to aid the project. At New Salem, Abraham Lincoln and others joined the axmen who were to clear the Sangamon of obstructions. The **Talisman** arrived at Beardstown March 9 and, after a 4-day delay due to ice, began the 100-mile trip to the Sangamon. When they arrived at Portland Landing, three-fourths of a mile east of here, on March 24 crowds greeted them and continued the celebration in Springfield for several days. Rowan Herndon was hired as pilot and Lincoln as assistant pilot for the return trip to Beardstown. Since the Sangamon was falling rapidly, the steamboat had to be backed partway downstream and at New Salem a section of the dam was removed to float the boat across.

When the boat reached Beardstown, Lincoln received $40 for his services from March 13 to April 6 and walked back to New Salem. The **Talisman** venture was financially unsuccessful and hopes for a river port near Springfield were eventually abandoned.

Located: On US 36 at Camp Butler National Cemetery, east of Springfield.

Camp Butler, shown above, was a Civil War prison camp for captured Confederates.

CAMP BUTLER

Camp Butler, Civil War concentration camp for Illinois Volunteers, occupied a large area in this vicinity from 1861 to 1866. It was also a prison camp for captured Confederates. Now a national cemetery, it contains the graves of 1642 Confederate and Union soldiers.

Located: Lincoln Depot, Monroe & 10th Sts., Springfield.

Lincoln depot, Springfield.

THE LINCOLN DEPOT

From this building on February 11, 1861, Abraham Lincoln departed Springfield, Illinois to assume the presidency of the United States. After bidding farewell to a number of friends, he delivered a brief, spontaneous and moving farewell address to the crowd, estimated at 1,000, from the rear platform of the train.

160

CLAYSVILLE

This building, one of the first brick buildings in Sangamon County, was built in the spring of 1834 by John Broadwell. His father, Moses Broadwell, a native of Elizabethtown, New Jersey, came to Illinois in 1820. He and his son John built a brick kiln and ran a tannery where animal skins were cured at this spot. Several buildings were constructed about 1824, however the present one is all that remains.

Between the 1830's and the early 1850's a stage line ran between Springfield and Beardstown. Tradition indicates that Eastern cattle buyers and cattle drovers heading for distant markets as well as teamsters hauling dry goods, liquor, groceries, hardware, and clothing between Beardstown on the Illinois River and Springfield traveled this route. Families of settlers spent the night here before seeking property for themselves. While the original inn burned in the late 1800's, the present brick building, notable in its time, was used to accommodate overflow crowds and it is possible that stage passengers, cattlemen, teamsters, and settlers shared experiences here.

The Broadwell's named this area Claysville in honor of Henry Clay, the leading Whig politician and this property was the scene of Whig festivities and poll-raisings. On the 4th of July, 1842, many Whigs met here for a celebration including speeches, music, marching, dining, and drinking. With the coming of the railroad and the rerouting of commerce and travel, Claysville passed into history.

Located: South side Ill. 125, 13 miles northwest of Springfield in front of "Clayville Tavern".

The Claysville Tavern.

State of Illinois, Department of Conservation

OFFICIAL STATE MAP: H-5
SANGAMON COUNTY

LINCOLN HOME NATIONAL HISTORIC SITE

Abraham Lincoln came to Springfield on April 15, 1837, as the law partner of John Todd Stuart. Though Lincoln was a new resident of Springfield, he was not a stranger to the town. Since 1834, he had represented Sangamon County in the Illinois General Assembly and helped to move the capital from Vandalia to Springfield. The prairie city was growing rapidly. A newspaperman wrote in 1839 that Springfield contained "a throng of stores, taverns and shops...an agreeable assemblage of dwelling houses very neatly painted, most of them white, and situated somewhat retiringly behind tasteful frontyards."

For Lincoln, the young lawyer and up-and-coming state legislator, Springfield possessed opportunities which could only enhance his already promising future. Here Lincoln could meet politicians and local leaders from all over the state. One was Stephen A. Douglas, a state senator who defeated Lincoln in the 1858 election for the U.S. Senate and whom, among others, Lincoln defeated for the Presidency in 1860. And here he met Mary Todd, his wife-to-be.

Mary Todd came from a prominent family. She was born in Lexington, Kentucky, on December 13, 1818, the daughter of Robert Smith Todd, president of the Bank of Kentucky. She grew up amid all the comforts which the times and area offered; she went to private schools which only children of the "best families" attended, and slaves waited on her. Her family and the society in which she moved put great stress on one's upbringing and family. In short, she grew up in much different surroundings than did the man who became her husband. And when she and Lincoln decided to marry, her family found it difficult to accept.

Mary Todd came to Springfield in 1839 to live with her sister, Elizabeth, who was married to Ninian Wirt Edwards, the son of a former governor of Illinois. A cousin of Mary Todd was Lincoln's law partner, and it is likely that this connection led to an introduction. Their relationship waxed and waned as the months passed but in the fall of 1842 they decided to marry.

The Lincoln home in Springfield.

Illinois State Historical Library

OFFICIAL STATE MAP: H-5
SANGAMON COUNTY

Located: Lincoln Home, Springfield.

Artist's conception of how Lincoln's home appeared before the second story was added.

On the morning of November 4, 1842, Lincoln went to the home of Dr. Charles Dresser, the Episcopal minister, and told him, "I want to get hitched tonight." Lincoln and Mary wanted to be married in the minister's home because of her family's opposition. But when her family found out that she was determined to go through with it, they relented and the ceremony took place in the Edwards' home that night.

The Lincolns began their married life in Springfield's Globe Tavern. Room and board cost them $4.00 a week. Here on August 1, 1843, Robert Todd Lincoln was born. He was the first of four sons and the only one to grow to manhood.

The Lincolns soon found that a boardinghouse was not a good place to raise a child, and on January 7, 1844, Lincoln signed a contract to buy the Rev. Charles Dresser's house at Eighth and Jackson Streets. Lincoln gave Dresser $1,200 in cash and a lot valued at $300.

The house was built in 1839 and is typical of that period. It was a one-and-a-half story building until 1856, when the Lincolns raised it to two stories. Wooden pegs and handmade nails hold together the native hardwood and white pine.

In this house the other three Lincoln children were born: Edward Baker, on March 10, 1840; William Wallace, December 21, 1850; and Thomas, April 4, 1853. Here too, their second son died on February 1, 1950.

When the Lincolns left for Washington in 1861, they sold their household furnishings. Many pieces were burned in the Chicago fire of 1871 and others have been lost. Some furniture, however, has been recovered and is now in the home.

The State of Illinois, which previously administered the site, was assisted in its restoration work by the Abraham Lincoln Association of Springfield and the National Society of the Colonial Dames of America in Illinois.

Lincoln's home in Springfield in the fall of 1865 showing remnants of mourning crepe.

LINCOLN'S TOMB STATE MEMORIAL

On the night of April 14, 1865, President Abraham Lincoln was shot in the back of the head by John Wilkes Booth at the Ford Theatre, Washington, D.C. The unconscious President was carried across the street to a bedroom in the Peterson house, where he died at 7:22 the following morning.

Abraham Lincoln was buried in Oak Ridge Cemetery at the request of Mrs. Lincoln on May 4, 1865. The Lincolns admired the beauty of the Springfield cemetery which was dedicated in 1860. Lincoln's body was placed in a public vault at the foot of the hill north of the tomb. This vault may still be seen. On December 21, 1865, the coffin was taken into a temporary vault on the hillside northeast of the tomb.

At the time of Lincoln's death the governor of Illinois, Richard J. Oglesby, requested the people of Springfield to form as association to raise funds to build a memorial to the memory of President Lincoln. The National Lincoln Monument Association was formed by about fifteen prominent citizens of Springfield with Governor Oglesby as its chairman. Solicitation of funds was begun with a goal of $240,000. A prize of $1,000 was offered for the design that the association members would deem most suitable. The design chosen was submitted by sculptor Larkin G. Mead of Brattleboro, Vermont.

Ground for the construction of the memorial was broken in 1869, four years after Lincoln's death. The tomb was dedicated on October 15, 1874. The cost of the tomb was $180,000. The National Lincoln Monument Association maintained the tomb until 1895 at which time Richard Oglesby, the sole surviving member of the original association, deeded the property to the State of Illinois.

On September 19, 1871, the remains of President Lincoln and sons Edward and William, who had preceded their father in death, were taken from the temporary vault and placed in crypts in the inner wall of the uncompleted tomb. On October 9, 1874, a few days before the formal

The temporary vault where Abraham Lincoln was buried in Oak Ridge Cemetery in May of 1865.

Illinois State Historical Library

OFFICIAL STATE MAP H-5
SANGAMON COUNTY

Located: Lincoln Tomb, Springfield.

Lincoln's Tomb as it is today.
Illinois State Historical Library

dedication of the tomb, Lincoln's coffin was placed in a white marble sarcophagus resting on the floor in the center of the burial chamber. An unsuccessful attempt was made on November 7, 1876, to steal the body of Lincoln for a hoped for $200,000 ransom. The conspirators were captured and at their trial were sentenced to one year terms in the penitentiary.

Immediately following the attempted theft. Lincoln's coffin was removed from the sarcophagus and secreted within the deep recesses of the tomb. On October 14, 1887. the coffin and that of Mrs. Lincoln, who had died on July 16. 1882. were placed in a brick vault constructed under the floor of the burial chamber. The marble sarcophagus was left in its position on the floor but the public was not informed that it no longer contained the remains of President Lincoln.

Due to the uneven settling of the earth under the tomb, a complete reconstruction of the structure was found to be necessary in 1899. Work was started at once and on September 26, 1901, the project was finished. The tomb was rededicated June 1, 1902.

Following the completion of this reconstruction Robert Todd Lincoln, the oldest son, requested that his father's body be placed in a specially designed steel and concrete vault beneath the floor of the chamber. Before lowering the coffin into the vault, it was opened and Lincoln's features were exposed to the view of a number of former friends and associates for the purpose of identification. Positive identification was established and signed affidavits were placed in the office of the secretary of state for preservation. Due to external and internal deterioration, the tomb was again reconstructed. Work began in 1930 and was completed in 1931. One June 17, 1931, President Herbert H oover arrived and delivered the dedicatory address to the thousands gathered for the ceremony. During the second reconstruction the tomb was completely remodeled.

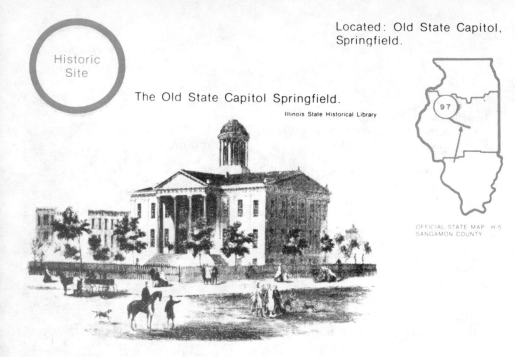

Located: Old State Capitol, Springfield.

Historic Site

The Old State Capitol Springfield.

Illinois State Historical Library

OFFICIAL STATE MAP H-5
SANGAMON COUNTY

THE OLD STATE CAPITOL

The Old State Capitol, Illinois' fifth statehouse, was the first one located in Springfield. In 1837, the Sangamon County legislators, led by Abraham Lincoln, sponsored the bill which changed the seat of government from Vandalia to Springfield.

The Greek Revival structure was designed by John F. Rague of Springfield. Construction on the foundation of locally quarried limestone began in June, 1837. The stone proved so attractive it was used for the entire building, rather than the brick originally specified.

Governor Thomas Carlin ordered the state offices moved to Springfield in July, 1839, and the legislature was able to move into the new Capitol in December, 1840. The building, which cost approximately $260,000, was officially completed in 1853.

After the Civil War, the Capitol was too small to house the legislature as well as the state administrative offices and supreme court. A new statehouse was authorized in 1867, and was ready for occupancy in 1876.

The Old State Capitol is open daily from 9 a.m. to 5 p.m. The museum is the county courthouse until 1965. In 1899, the county needed more space, so the building was jacked up, adding a new first floor and rebuilding the interior.

Over the years, a number of solutions were posed for preserving the building, and in 1961 it was repurchased by the state. Because of the major alterations made by the county, and because modern utilities had to be incorporated into the structure, reconstruction was deemed the most feasible method of making the building look as it did during Lincoln's era. This solution also allowed for the construction of a new underground State Historical Library and parking garage on the site.

All the exterior stones were saved and reapplied over a new skeleton of concrete and steel. The Old State Capitol was rededicated on December 3,

The House of Representatives, Old State Capitol, Springfield.

Illinois State Historical Library

1968, and after being furnished with antiques purchased by the Abraham Lincoln Association, was opened to the public on November 15, 1969.
The Old StateCapitol is open daily from 9 a.m. to 5 p.m. The museum is closed on Thanksgiving, Christmas, and New Year's Day.

President-Elect Abraham Lincoln receiving visitors in the Governor's Room in the Old State Capitol in Springfield.

Illinois State Historical Library

LINDBERGH FIELD

Springfield's first airport, developed by the chamber of commerce, was located on this 35-acre tract of land. In April 1926, Charles A. Lindbergh, chief pilot for Robertson Aircraft, St. Louis, assisted in selecting the field. He flew mail to Springfield on the St. Louis-Chicago route until he began preparing for his solo trans-Atlantic flight of May 20, 1927. On August 15 of that year the field was named in his honor. It was used until 1929.

Charles Lindbergh on right.

Illinois State Historical Library

Located: North of Intersection Ill. 97-125, northwest of Springfield.

OFFICIAL STATE MAP: H-5
SANGAMON COUNTY

PETER CARTWRIGHT

Near Pleasant Plains the famous Methodist circuit rider, Peter Cartwright, made his home from 1824 until his death in 1872. His powerful preaching led many thousands into the church, and made him a dominant figure in the religious life of Illinois for half a century.

OFFICIAL STATE MAP: H-5
SANGAMON COUNTY

Located: North side of Rt. 125 in Pleasant Plains.

Illinois State Historical Library

The famous Methodist minister and circuit rider, Peter Cartwright, who was defeated by Lincoln in the congressional elections of 1846.

OFFICIAL STATE MAP G-2
SCHUYLER COUNTY

Located: Near Huntsville.

Illinois State Historical Library

Dorsey grave.

ABRAHAM LINCOLN'S TEACHER

Azel Waters Dorsey, 1784-1858, teacher of Abraham Lincoln, is buried on the King farm one mile south of Huntsville. Dorsey taught a "blab school" in Spencer County, Indiana which young Lincoln attended for six months in 1824. He moved to Schuyler County, Illinois in 1828 where he taught school.

169

THE BASE LINE SURVEY

Nearby is one of two sites in Illinois which serve as the basis for all land surveys in the state. Just northwest of Beardstown, the 4th Principal Meridian intersects its base line.

Originally, land was measured by "Metes and Bounds." Known landmarks were the points of reference. Boundary lines were compass lines or natural boundaries such as streams. This system proved unsatisfactory since landmarks are changeable and compass lines can vary. In May, 1785, Congress adopted the "Rectangular System" of land measurement. In each state or group of states one of more north-south principal meridians and one or more east-west base lines on parallels of latitude are established at right angles to one another. These lines are determined by astronomical observation and numbered. The 3rd and 4th Principal Meridians intersect their respective base lines in Illinois and govern all land measurements in the state.

Parallel lines are calculated at six mile intervals east and west through each principal meridian's territory. These divisions, called ranges, are consecutively numbered in each direction from the meridian. Similar lines parallel to the base line mark divisions called townships. The six mile squares created by the intersecting lines form government townships. The

170

number and direction of the township and range lines such as Range 2 West, Township 3 North, locate any township in relation to its principal meridian. Government townships are broken down into 36 numbered sections containing 640 acres. Acres form the basis of most property identification.

Base Line Survey map.

OFFICIAL STATE MAP   H-4
SCHUYLER COUNTY

Located: U.S. 67, northwest of Beardstown.

OFFICIAL STATE MAP: I-3
SCOTT COUNTY

Located: Rest area, U.S. 36-54, 5 miles northeast of Winchester.

Illinois State Historical Library

The reception of Judge Douglas at Chicago, October 4, 1860.

STEPHEN ARNOLD DOUGLAS

Stephen A. Douglas was born in Brandon, Vermont, in 1813. He attended schools there and in New York state. In 1833 he settled in Winchester, Illinois, five miles southwest, where he taught school. In 1834 he moved to Jacksonville, eight miles northeast of here, and began to practice law.

He soon became a leader of the Democratic Party in Illinois. He was elected representative to the state legislature in 1836, appointed Illinois secretary of state in 1840, and elected judge of the state supreme court in 1841.

After moving to Quincy, Douglas served as a representative in Congress from 1843 to 1847. He changed his residence to Chicago in 1847 and served in the United States Senate from 1847 until his death in 1861.

As an expansionist, Douglas favored acquisition of Oregon to 54' 40' North Latitude, annexation of Texas led to the Mexican War and American acquisition of new western lands. The bills to organize this area into territories were included in the Compromise of 1850. Embodied in these bills and the Kansas-Nebraska Act, which Douglas introduced in 1854, was the doctrine of "Popular Sovereignty"--the idea that the people in each territory could decide the issue of slavery for themselves.

In the debates of the 1858 campaign, Abraham Lincoln asked Douglas to reconcile "Popular Sovereignty" and the Supreme Court decision that slavery could not be barred from the territories. In reply Douglas advanced the Freeport Doctrine: That slavery could be excluded by local legislation. Douglas kept the Senate seat but lost southern support for his presidential candidacy in 1860.

THOMPSON MILL BRIDGE

This bridge, which spans the Kaskaskia River, is on a road that once was an important route from Springfield to Effingham. The bridge was completed in the autumn of 1868 at the cost of $2,500 and named for the owner of the first mill at this location. It is the narrowest of eight remaining nineteenth-century covered wooden bridges in Illinois, being only 10 feet 7 inches wide. The height is 11 feet 4 inches. The bridge is carried on each side by a Howe truss 105 feet long. Each of the panels of the truss consists of a vertical iron tension rod and two diagonal wooden compression members that form an X.

Illinois State Historical Library

Located: Twp. road 389, N.E. of Cowden.

OFFICIAL STATE MAP: J-7
SHELBY COUNTY

The Thompson Mill bridge, built in 1868, is the narrowest of eight remaining covered wooden bridges in Illinois.

Located: on Rt. 29 (LaSalle Ave) at junction of gravel road (Park Road) to Fort Crevecoeur State Park in Creve Coeur. Placed in southwest corner of the intersection.

OFFICIAL STATE MAP: F-5
TAZEWELL COUNTY

FORT DE CREVECOEUR

Overlooking the Illinois River one-quarter mile to the west, La Salle and Tonti erected Fort de Crevecoeur, the first public building in Illinois. Built early in 1680, Fort de Crevecoeur was damaged by its mutinous garrison in April of that year and was never rebuilt. The site is now a state park.

OFFICIAL STATE MAP F-5
TAZEWELL COUNTY

Located: 108 East Washington, Tremont.

Illinois State Historical Library

Lincoln, probably April 1858.

TREMONT COURTHOUSE, 1839-1850

Abraham Lincoln attended court in the fine two story rectangular brick courthouse with four Grecian columns and copper dome on this site. Here in 1842 he was challenged to a duel by James Shields. Lincoln last spoke here August 30, 1858.

OFFICIAL STATE MAP F-5
TAZEWELL COUNTY

Located: On 333 Court St., Pekin National Bank Bldg., Pekin.

UNION LEAGUE OF AMERICA

On June 25, 1862, the Union League of America was founded at Pekin, Illinois, to promote patriotism and loyalty to the Union. Its members hoped to counter northern disillusionment with President Lincoln's military policies after early Union defeats in the Civil War. Although closely allied with the Republican Party, the league sought to enroll all Union supporters, regardless of party. The league developed into a statewide and then a national organization. By December, 1863, it claimed 140,000 members in Illinois and almost a million nationwide. After the war, the league councils in the South were concerned with franchising the Negro and working for their education.

Located: North side of US 136, 1.8 miles East of Danville.

THY WONDROUS STORY, ILLINOIS

The fertile prairies in Illinois attracted the attention of French trader Louis Jolliet and Father Jacques Marquette as they explored the Mississippi and Illinois Rivers in 1673. France claimed this region until 1763 when she surrendered it to Great Britian by the Treaty of Paris. During the American Revolution George Rogers Clark and his small army scored a bloodless victory when they captured Kaskaskia for the Commonwealth of Virginia, and Illinois became a county of Virginia. This area was ceded to the United States in 1784, and became in turn a part of the Northwest Territory and the Indiana and Illinois territories. On December 3, 1818, Illinois entered the Union as the twenty-first state.

The prairies bordering Highway 136 from here to the Illinois River were among the last settled sections in Illinois. The early pioneers preferred timbered tracts along the rivers and creeks or areas of special importance such as the salines west of Danville where wild life, Indians, and, by 1819 settlers came for salt. The tall, sweet grass, however, made the prairies an ideal area for the cattle industry and after 1835 enterprising men fattened large herds for sale in eastern markets. Eventually purebred stock replaced the frontier breeds and corn, raised by the cattle kings, replaced the grass. From 1862 to 1873 high prices and low costs brought net returns which made some cattle kings millionaires. As late as the 1880's the corn belt maintained more cattle than the great plains.

An Illinois Sesquicentennial painting of Marquette and Joliet discovering Illinois.

174

OFFICIAL STATE MAP: F-6
WOODFORD COUNTY

Located: Eastbound Rest area. I-74. west of Bloomington.

David Davis, from a daguerreotype taken about 1846.

DAVID DAVIS

David Davis. a distinguished Illinois jurist, was born in Maryland in 1815. He graduated from Kenyon College in Ohio and studied law at Yale. In 1836 he settled at Bloomington, Illinois, which was his home town the remainder of his life.

From the commonplace activities of a pioneer lawyer, Davis turned to politics and was elected as a Whig to the Lower House of the Illinois Legislature in 1844. Three years later he served in the State Constitutional Convention.

In 1848 he was elected judge of the State's Eighth Judicial Circuit, then comprised of fourteen Central Illinois counties. He served until 1862. Many lawyers of distinction, including Abraham Lincoln, practiced before him. During this time he and Lincoln became warm friends. Lincoln at times presided over the court when the judge was absent

Davis organized the forces that nominated Lincoln in the Republican National Convention at Chicago in 1860 and then campaigned vigorously for Lincoln's election. Two years later Lincoln appointed Davis to the Supreme Court of the United States.

During the 1870's, Davis disassociated himself from partisan affairs, establishing his reputation as a political independent. In 1877 he resigned from the court after being elected to the United States Senate by the Illinois Legislature. He served as president pro tempore from 1881 to 1883. He then retired to "Clover Lawn," his victorian mansion in Bloomington, where he died in 1886. His mansion, at Monroe and Davis Streets. now preserved by the Illinois State Historical Library, is open to the public.

METAMORA COURT HOUSE

As a member of the traveling bar of the Eighth Judicial Circuit, Lincoln came twice a year to Metamora, then the seat of Woodford County, to attend court in the courthouse which faces the north side of this park. David Davis, Robert G. Ingersoll and Adlai E. Stevenson were others who practiced here.

Located: Southeast corner of park in place of wooden marker: faces State Rt. 116. NW corner E. Mt. Vernon (Ill. 116) & S. Davenport Sts. on N side of 116.

OFFICIAL STATE MAP: F-6
WOODFORD COUNTY

Metamora Courthouse.

NORTHERN
ILLINOIS

Stephen A. Hurlbut.

OFFICIAL STATE MAP: B-7
BOONE COUNTY

Located: Southeast corner of East Hurlbut Ave. and North State St., Belvidere.

MARKER MISSING

GENERAL STEPHEN A. HURLBUT
1815-1882

Born South Carolina, admitted to bar 1837. Came to Belvidere 1845. Member Illinois Constitutional 1847. State House of Representatives 1859-61, 1867. In Civil War 1861-65. Brig. Gen. Volunteers 1861. Maj. Gen. Volunteers 1862. First National Commander G.A.R. 1866-68. Minister Colombia 1869-72. Congressman 1873-77. Minister Peru 1881-82. Buried in Belvidere Cemetery.

CHERRY MINE DISASTER

Just north of town are remnants of the Cherry Coal Mine, where 259 miners lost their lives in one of the worst mine disasters in United States history.

The St. Paul Coal Company began mining coal at Cherry in 1905 and by 1909 was mining 300,000 tons annually. The owner and sole customer was the Chicago, Milwaukee, and St. Paul Railroad.

On Saturday, November 13, 1909, the mine caught fire. A load of hay, intended for the mule stables at the bottom of the mine, was apparently ignited by burning oil dripping from a kerosene torch. The fire spread rapidly. Several miners reached safety; others were trapped in the mine. Twenty-one of the trapped men were later rescued. The remainder died in the mine. The dead included twelve rescuers.

Public response to the needs of the victims was great. Individuals and organizations from various communities donated time and money. Chicago and other towns sent fire-fighting men and equipment. More than $400,000 in relief funds was raised, and the Cherry Relief Commission was organized to distribute the funds.

Another $400,000 was added as a result of the settlement made with the railroad company. John E. Williams of Streator, vice chairman of the Cherry Relief Commission, acted as mediator between the relatives of the miners and the company.

The disaster prompted the state legislature to establish stricter regulations for mine safety and to pass a Workmen's Compensation Act, making an employer liable even when there is contributory negligence.

Located: Ill 89, Village park, Cherry.

Cherry Mine Disaster.

OFFICIAL STATE MAP: D-6
BUREAU COUNTY

Illinois State Historical Library

179

From: LIVES AND TIMES OF ARCHY MEHITABEL by Doubleday Publishing Co.

Located: Ill. 92, west of Walnut.

OFFICIAL STATE MAP: D-6
BUREAU COUNTY

DON MARQUIS

Don Marquis, American humorist, dramatist, and poet, was born in Walnut, July 29, 1878. In 1899 he went to Washington, D.C., where he began his career in journalism. He later worked on newspapers in Atlanta and New York City. In Atlanta he also wrote with Joel Chandler Harris for **Uncle Remus' Magazine.** In a column called the "Sun Dial," which he wrote for the **New York Evening Sun** from 1913 to 1922, he created fictional characters whose conversations and antics expressed the author's commentaries on the times. The most popular characters were Archy, a literary cockroach, and Mehitabel, rowdy queen of the alley cats. Marquis died in 1937. His principal works number more than twenty-five.

JOHN MITCHELL
1870-1919

Pioneer resident of Spring Valley. Achieved national prominence in the settlement of the Pennsylvania anthracite miners strike in 1902 with the co-operation of President Theodore Roosevelt.

President of United Mine Workers, 1889-1908. Author of two widely-read books on union recognition. Often acclaimed as an enlightened and fair minded labor leader.

OFFICIAL STATE MAP D-6
BUREAU COUNTY

OFFICIAL STATE MAP: D-6
BUREAU COUNTY

OFFICIAL STATE MAP: D-6
BUREAU COUNTY

Located: (1) Intersection of May St. and East Dakota St. (US 6E). Spring Valley. (2) Intersection Strong Ave. and West Dakota St. (US 6W), Spring Valley. (3) Intersection Caroline St. and South Spaulding St. (Ill. 89 S), Spring Valley.

John Mitchell and family at home, Dec. 15, 1902.

OFFICIAL STATE MAP   D-6
BUREAU COUNTY

Located: Lovejoy Home,
Princeton.

Owen Lovejoy.

OWEN LOVEJOY HOME

This two-story frame structure was the home of abolitionist Owen Lovejoy. who was born in Maine in 1811. Lovejoy moved into the house in 1838. when he became a Congregationalist minister. He was a leader in the formation of the Republican Party in Illinois, and he served as a representative in the State Legislature, 1855-1857, and in the United States Congress from 1857 until his death in 1864. His home was well known as a shelter for runaway slaves. Owen was a younger brother of Elijah Lovejoy, who was killed by a mob at Alton in 1837.

HELEN SCOTT HAY

Helen Scott Hay, famous Red Cross nurse, was born near Lanark in this county. She was a graduate of Savanna High School, Northwestern University in Evanston, and the Illinois Training School for Nurses in Chicago, where she was later superintendent. Before World War I she helped establish a school of nursing in Bulgaria. At the outbreak of war she became Director of American Red Cross nursing personnel and was assigned to the Balkans. After America entered the war, she served in Washington. In 1920 she was appointed Director of the European Work of the Red Cross. She died here in 1932.

Located: III. 84, American Legion Post 148, Chicago Avenue and Fourth, Savanna.

OFFICIAL STATE MAP B-4
CARROLL COUNTY

American Red Cross workers in WW I from ALBUM OF AMERICAN HISTORY, Vol. 5, p. 5.

Illinois State Historical Library

WE the undersigned having been appointed by an order of the County Commissioners' Court of Fulton County, to Survey, View and Mark out a road from the mouth of Spoon river, to the Lead Mines on Fever river, do hereby certify that we have performed the same, and fixed the route much better than we expected, and nearly on a direct north line. At least nine tenths of the distance is dry prairie, and no large creeks, bad swamps or hills on the route. We leave the great Winnebago swamp entirely to the east, and cross the outlet of the same, which is a handsome stream with a gravelly bottom, and good fording; and cross Rock river at the old Sock town, about thirty miles from the Mississippi, and intersects the prairie trace about 15 miles north from Rock river. Five large loaded wagons immediately followed our trace through, and a number of other waggons have since been thro' without any difficulty. We are also authorised to state that a road will immediately be opened from the mouth of Spoon river, the most direct route to Sangamon court-house, crossing the Sangamon river below the mouth of Salt creek. We do not hesitate to say that this route is much nearer and on better ground for a road than any other route which has or can be obtained without considerable expense.

We also recommend this as the best route for travellers from Peoria to follow the old Indian trace to where it intersects our road, in 19 N. 3 E. as by so doing they will shun all the bad swamps, and cross Rock river where there are some Sock Indians, who are more friendly than the Winnebagoes, and the river can be forded in low water.

Distance from Sangamon Court	Miles.
House to Sangamon town,	7
To the ferry on Sangamon river	20
Illinois Ferry,	18
Lewistown,	8
Briton's, 7 N 3 E	14
Spoon river, 9 N 3 E.	13
Court creek, 11 N 3 E.	10
Colter's creek, 13 N 3 E.	14
Walnut creek, 14 N. 3 E.	8
Prairie creek 15 N. 3 E.	6
Outlet of Winnebago swamp,	12
Sock village on Rock river,	20
Peoria trace,	15
Plum river,	20
Apple river,	12
Lead Mines,	14
	205

OSSIAN M. ROSS.
JOHN HOLCOMB.
SHELDEN LOCKWOOD.
March 16, 1817

OFFICIAL STATE MAP: B-4
CARROLL COUNTY

Located: U.S. 52 & Ill. 64,
east of Savanna.

Road viewers' report, ILLINOIS INTELLIGENCER, March 31, 1827.

LEWISTOWN TRAIL

Lewistown Trail ran from Springfield to Galena via Lewistown. From 1827 to 1837 it was one of the main routes to the Galena lead mines. In general the trail ran in a northerly direction, crossing the Rock River at Prophetstown. It then zigzagged over the glaciated slopes of Carroll County and at this point turned northward again toward Plum River, six miles away. In 1837 when a state road was established to Galena via Savanna, this portion of the old trail became a local wagon road. By the 1850's it was a post road to the mill towns of Jacobsville and Polsgrove.

Located: Old Mill Park, east
of Savanna.

PLUM RIVER FALLS

Steamboats once navigated to this point, where Plum River Falls powered saw, powder, grist, and flour mills at various times between 1836 and 1885. Near here the Rock Island Military and Prophetstown Trails to Galena were intersected as early as the 1830's by roads to Freeport, Rockford, Polo, and Milledgeville. On three occasions during the Black Hawk War, companies of mounted volunteers from Galena scoured this area for hostile Indians.

Savanna, Illinois.
Illinois State Historical Library

185

Shimer College.

Located: Shimer campus drive, Mount Carroll.

OFFICIAL STATE MAP: B-4
CARROLL COUNTY

SHIMER COLLEGE

Mount Carroll Seminary was founded as a coeducational institution in 1853 by Frances Ann Wood (later Mrs. Shimer). After the Civil War, enrollment was limited to women, Rechartered in 1896 as the Frances Shimer Academy of the University of Chicago, the school pioneered a junior college program. It became coeducational again in 1950 and adopted a four-year program in liberal education in 1958. In that year the Chicago affiliation was dissolved and the present name became official.

186

A STONE ARCH BRIDGE ON THE GALENA ROAD

The Stone Arch Bridge that stands to the east of the present highway was on the Galena Road, once the most important trail in Northern Illinois. Along this route innumerable people streamed northward to the lead mines near Galena every spring and many returned southward in the fall. The movement was likened to that of the fish called Sucker, from which the state received its nickname.

This portion of the road from Dixon was surveyed in 1830 as the road from Woodbine Springs to Ogee's Ferry (later Dixon's Ferry, now Dixon), replacing the longer 1825 Kellogg's Trail and the 1826 Boles' Trail. Roads from Peoria and Chicago joined at Dixon and continued as one to Galena. Mail and stagecoach lines traveled the Peoria-Galena route as early as 1830 and the Chicago-Galena route by 1834. Here the road intersected the earlier Gratiot's Trail, which also ran from Dixon to Galena but extended farther north to avoid the rough terrain.

During the Black Hawk War in 1832 militia and regular army troops marched on both trails. Abraham Lincoln, as a private in the company of Captain Elijah Iles, camped overnight near here, June 8 and 12. As a private in the independent spy company of Jacob M. Early, Lincoln made a forced march to Kellogg's Grove (near Kent), arriving there June 26, the day after the last battle fought in Illinois during that war.

Isaac Chambers, who was not only the first settler of Ogle County at Buffalo Grove near Polo but also of Lima Township here in Carroll County, operated a stagecoach inn nearby and a sawmill on Elkhorn Creek two miles to the southeast.

OFFICIAL STATE MAP: B-4
CARROLL COUNTY

Located: rest area on U.S. 52-Ill. 64, 1½ mi. northwest of Brookville.

BLACK HAWK CAMPAIGN

ATKINSON'S ROUTE
BLACK HAWK'S ROUTE

Illinois State Historical Library

This map of the Black Hawk Campaign shows the Galena Road (dotted line) and marks many of the large battles.

Illinois acquired the fourteen northern counties because of the foresight of Nathaniel Pope, congressional delegate from the Illinois territory, shown above.

OFFICIAL STATE MAP: B-4
CARROLL COUNTY

Located: South side of US 52-64, 1.2 miles east of Savanna.

THY WONDROUS STORY, ILLINOIS

SEE HISTORIC ILLINOIS

The fertile prairies in Illinois attracted the attention of French trader Louis Jolliet and Father Jacques Marquette as they explored the Mississippi and Illinois Rivers in 1673. France claimed this region until 1763 when she surrendered it to Great Britain by the Treaty of Paris. During the American Revolution George Rogers Clark and his small army scored a bloodless victory when they captured Kaskaskia for the Commonwealth of Virginia, and Illinois became a county of Virginia. This area was ceded to the United States in 1784, and became in turn a part of the Northwest Territory and the Indiana and Illinois territories. On December 3, 1818, Illinois entered the Union as the twenty-first state.

Illinois acquired the fourteen northern counties because of the foresight of Nathaniel Pope, congressional delegate from the Illinois Territory. His amendment to the Statehood Act moved the upper boundary from an east-west line through the tip of Lake Michigan to the present location.

US 52 passes a variety of scenic and historic sites. The Mississippi Palisades, north of Savanna, and the White Pines forest, east of Polo, preserve the natural beauty of the area. In Dixon the statue of Abraham Lincoln as a soldier in the Black Hawk War and in the Lowden State Park near Oregon the towering Indian statue recall the exciting year 1832 when a band of Sauk and Fox Indians terrorized the settlers in northern Illinois.

THE GREEN BAY TRAIL

One branch of the Green Bay Trail traversed this region. Originally an Indian trail, after 1816 the route connected Fort Dearborn at Chicago with Fort Howard at Green Bay. Couriers faced hunger, cold and Indians to carry dispatches on a round trip which took a month.

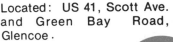

OFFICIAL STATE MAP: B-9
COOK COUNTY

Located: US 41, Scott Ave. and Green Bay Road, Glencoe.

HAYMARKET RIOT

On May 4, 1886, hundreds of workers gathered here to protest police action of the previous day against strikers engaged in a nationwide campaign for an eight-hour work day. Radicals addressed the crowd. When police attempted to disperse the rally, someone threw a bomb. The bomb and ensuing pistol shots killed seven policemen and four other persons. Although no evidence linked the radicals to the bomb, eight of them were convicted and four hanged. Three were later pardoned. The strike collapsed after the tragedy.

OFFICIAL STATE MAP: C-10
COOK COUNTY

Located: Haymarket Square, Randolph & Des p l a i n e s Streets, Chicago.

Illinois State Historical Library
Police dispersing the crowd at Haymarket Square in Chicago, May 4, 1886.   189

STATE MEMORIAL

THE DOUGLAS TOMB STATE MEMORIAL

Stephen A. Douglas is revered in many ways in Illinois and across the nation. Many portraitures and statues of Douglas are at various Lincoln shrines because of the famous Lincoln-Douglas debates, which were bitter but there still was a feeling of admiration reaching to affection between the two men. The bronze statue of Douglas on the Capitol lawn in Springfield overshadows that of Lincoln.

Perhaps the most impressive and appropriate is the state memorial on the property Douglas chose in Chicago as the site for the home he had planned to build. The quiet, peaceful, pretty little park, generously sprinkled with colorful flowers in the summertime, seems to be the right place for the dignified "Little Giant"--the man who fought fiercely for his beliefs, but was as well-known for his gentle kindness.

The Douglas Tomb State Memorial soars in serene dignity in the center of a beautiful little park of 2.2 acres, an impressive memorial to Stephen A. Douglas.

Who was Douglas? Stephen Arnold Douglas was a man history pushed aside and forgot. He was 5 feet 4 inches tall, a fighting lawyer, a brave politician, a crusader for just plain people, a man who earned the nickname the "Little Giant" and was called that with profound respect and reverence.

Douglas in 1849, purchased a tract of 53 acres on the southern edge of Chicago, which he called "Oakenwald." In 1854 he expressed a willingness to help with the founding of Chicago University, not to be confused with the present University of Chicago. Two years later he deeded 10 acres to be used as a campus. He was elected president of the school and held that position during his lifetime.

The nation was stunned when Stephen A. Douglas died in Chicago, June 3, 1861. Illinois mourned the death of its first nationally known statesman. The body of the "Little Giant" lay in state in one of the

Illinois State Historical Library

The monument to Stephen A. Douglas in Chicago.

OFFICIAL STATE MAP:
COOK COUNTY

Located: Chicago.

A 1907 photograph of the Douglas home in Chicago.

university buildings and was then borne about 100 feet east of the campus near the Douglas cottage and buried under the tract of a primitive highway, one a stage road, within a few feet of the great railway of which he had been the chief promoter. This sixteen foot square was immediately enclosed by a crude, board fence.

The following October a group of his friends met in Chicago and organized the Douglas Monument Association. The purpose of this organization was to collect sufficient monies to erect and maintain a monument in Chicago in memory of Stephen A. Douglas. Leonard W. Volk, the well-known sculptor and a relative of Douglas by marriage, was commissioned to design the memorial.

The Douglas Cottage was deeded to the assocation by his mother and sister. Funds for the building of the tomb and momument were slow in amterializing. The state legislature failed to make an appropriation in 1863. Designer Volk sold photographs of the grave for $1.00 and a portrait of Douglas for $2.00 but he realized only $2,500. The governor was authorized in 1865 to purchase the property for the state as a tomb for Douglas and for

The sum of $25,000 was appropriated for the purchase and Mrs. Adele Douglas, his widow, conveyed the property to the state. On June 3, 1868, following the completion of the base of the memorial, Douglas' body was removed from the grave and placed in the sarcophagus. He is the only one buried there.

The Great Chicago Fire of 1871 destroyed Volk's designs. New appropriations of $50,000 were made in 1877 and $9,000 in 1879. Volk was awarded his last contract in 1880. The tom was considered complete May 5, 1881. The total cost was $90,000, of which $84,000 were state funds.

Stephen A. Douglas.

191

Illinois State Historical Library

Pullman, Illinois, looking east from the Arcade.

OFFICIAL STATE MAP C-10
COOK COUNTY

Located: 111th Street near Cottage Grove, Chicago.

PULLMAN

Pullman, first planned industrial town in the nation, was built in 1880-1884. This company town, conceived by George Pullman, inventor of the sleeping car, was designed by architect Solon Beman. In 1894 a strike at the Pullman Company was supported by Eugene Debs' Railway Union. After violence broke out, President Cleveland, over protests of Governor Altgeld, sent Federal troops to restore order. An injunction against the union broke the strike. In 1907 the town was annexed to Chicago.

Stephen A. Douglas.
Illinois State Historical Library

Located: O a k e n w a l d, Douglas' former estate, Chicago.

OFFICIAL STATE MAP C-10
COOK COUNTY

STEPHEN ARNOLD DOUGLAS
1813-1861

Stephen Arnold Douglas, one of the most distinguished statesmen of his day, was a justice of the Illinois Supreme Court, member of the House of Respresentatives, and United States Senator. Although a political rival of Lincoln, he supported the Union at the outbreak of the Civil War and contributed greatly to the solidarity of the North. This tomb stands in Oakenwald, Douglas' former estate.

192

THY WONDROUS STORY, ILLINOIS

SEE HISTORIC ILLINOIS

The fertile prairies in Illinois attracted the attention of French trader Louis Jolliet and Father Jacques Marquette as they explored the Mississippi and Illinois Rivers in 1673. France claimed this region until 1763 when she surrendered it to Great Britain by the Treaty of Paris. During the American Revolution George Rogers Clark and his small army scored a bloodless victory when they captured Kaskaskia for the Commonwealth of Virginia, and Illinois became a county of Virginia. This area was ceded to the United States in 1784, and became in turn a part of the Northwest Territory and the Indiana and Illinois territories. On December 3, 1818, Illinois entered the Union as the twenty-first state.

US 30 passes through historic territory. The old Sauk Trail roughly parallels US 30 from the Indiana line to Joliet. The Potawatomi hunted in this area for at least a century before the coming of the settlers. The Indians used hickory wood in making bows and arrows and camped frequently in the Hickory Creek area. Settlers came into this region in the 1820's and communities on or north of US 30 trace their origin to the Hickory Creek settlement.

An Indian village in the vicinity of Plainfield attracted Jesse Walker, pioneer Methodist circuit rider, in 1826. This dedicated missionary, known as "Father Walker" and as the "Daniel Boone of Methodism," held the first camp meeting in the state in 1807 near Edwardsville. He died in 1835 after a long and effective career. He is buried in Plainfield.

OFFICIAL STATE MAP: D-10
COOK COUNTY

Located: North side of US 30, 500 feet west of the junction with Illinois 83 near East Chicago Heights.

Momument to Jesse Walker.

193

Illinois State Historical Library

Lock on the Illinois & Michigan Canal, Channahon, Illinois.

Located: US 6, just west of the Indiana line, Calumet City.

THY WONDROUS STORY, ILLINOIS

SEE HISTORIC ILLINOIS

The fertile prairies in Illinois attracted the attention of French trader Louis Jolliet and Father Jacques Marquette as they explored the Mississippi and Illinois Rivers in 1673. France claimed this region until 1763 when she surrendered it to Great Britain by the Treaty of Paris. During the American Revolution George Rogers Clark and his small army scored a bloodless victory when they captured Kaskaskia for the Commonwealth of Virginia, and Illinois became a county of Virginia. This area was ceded to the United States in 1784, and became in turn a part of the Northwest Territory and the Indiana and Illinois Territories. On December 3, 1818, Illinois entered the Union as the twenty-first state.

US 6 parallels the Illinois River from its origin at the confluence of the Kankakee and Des Plaines Rivers to Peru. As early as 1673 Jolliet noted the desirability of a canal connecting Lake Michigan to the Mississippi via the Illinois.

By a treaty with the Potawatomi in 1816 the United States obtained a strip of land twenty miles wide along the Des Plaines and Illinois Rivers extending throughout the area. In 1836 construction of the Illinois and Michigan Canal was begun and was completed in 1848. The canal extended from the Chicago River along the course of the Des Plaines and Illinois Rivers to La Salle. It was an important trade link for thirty years but was eventually replaced by the railroads. Restored sections may be seen in Channahon and Gebhard Woods State Parks on US 6.

BARBED WIRE MANUFACTURING
1873-1938

This house, built in 1861, was the home of Joseph F. Glidden, who in 1873 invented barbed wire fencing. With Phineas W. Vaughn he perfected a machine to manufacture it. DeKalb was the home of Isaac L. Ellwood and Jacob Haish, also manufacturers of barbed wire. Haish developed the S-barb. DeKalb became the manufacturing center for barbed wire, significant in the development of the west.

Located: Glidden farm at DeKalb.

OFFICIAL STATE MAP: C-7
DEKALB COUNTY

Fence making machinery.

Illinois State Historical Library

Chief Shabbona, the white man's friend. He died in 1859.

OFFICIAL STATE MAP: C-7
DEKALB COUNTY

Located: On south side Rt. 30, at eastern edge of Shabbona.

SHABBONA'S VILLAGE

For many years Shabbona and his band lived in a large grove one-half mile to the south. Although he fought with the British in the War of 1812, Shabbona repeatedly risked his life during the Winnebago outbreak and the Black Hawk War to warn the settlers of northern Illinois of Indian dangers.

Located: Village Hall, Addison.

ARMY TRAIL ROAD

This road followed an Indian trail that began in Chicago and went through Du Page, Kane, De Kalb, Boone, and Winnebago counties to a Winnebago village at Beloit, Wisconsin. In August, 1832, during the Black Hawk War, United States Army reinforcements from the eastern department followed the trail. Their general, Winfield Scott, left Chicago ahead of the troops and took a different route to the war area. Delayed by chlorera, his men did not reach the front until after Black Hawk's defeat. The tracks left by heavy army wagons formed a road for early settlers.

Indian trails with villages and camps shown with Indian signs and markings.

Illinois State Historical Library

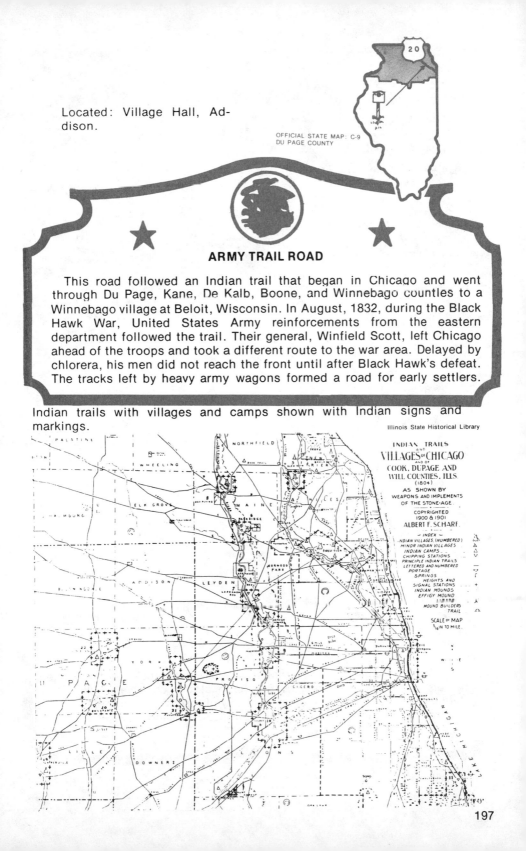

197

Fort Payne.

OFFICIAL STATE MAP: C-9
DU PAGE COUNTY

Located: US 34, near Merner Fieldhouse on North Central College Campus in Naperville.

FORT PAYNE

Near this site in 1832 a 100-foot square stockade enclosed by wooden pickets, with two blockhouses on diagonal corners, was built. Here Captain Morgan L. Payne and his company of forty-five men protected the settlers from roaming Sauk Indians during the Black Hawk War.

STACY'S TAVERN

Moses Stacy, solder in the War of 1812, arrived here in 1835. This inn, built in 1846 and his second home, was a halfway stop between Chicago and the Fox River Valley and a probable stage stop for Rockford-Galena coaches. For many years the village was called "Stacy's Corners."

Located: Geneva & Main,
Glen Ellyn.

OFFICIAL STATE MAP C-9
DU PAGE COUNTY

Stacy's Tavern.

Illinois State Historical Library

OFFICIAL STATE MAP: D-8
GRUNDY COUNTY

Located: On west side of III. 47 in Morris immediately north of canal.

ILLINOIS AND MICHIGAN CANAL

This historic artery of travel was commenced in 1836 and finished in 1848. By carrying pioneers and their produce between Lake Michigan and the Illinois Valley, it figured largely in the development of northern Illinois. Superseded by the Deep Waterway after fifty years of use, it is now devoted to recreational purposes.

This map shows the Illinois waterway between Peru-LaSalle and Lockport, Illinois.

Illinois State Historical Library

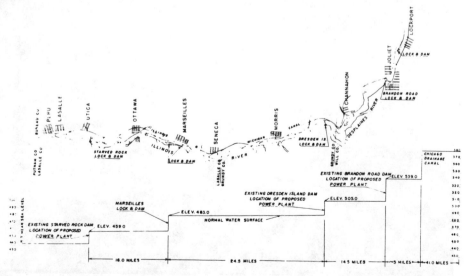

OFFICIAL STATE MAP: D-4
HENRY COUNTY

Located: Rest area, west side of Ill. 82, eight miles south of Cambridge.

Benjamin D. Walsh.

BENJAMIN DANN WALSH

Benjamin Dann Walsh, Illinois state entomologist from 1867 to 1869, was a pioneer in the application of insect study to agriculture. Born in England on September 21, 1808, he was intended for the ministry. However, he chose the literary field and wrote for newspapers and magazines for several years. A man of varied interests, he published a pamphlet on university reform and a translation of **The Comedies of Aristophanes.** In 1838 he married Rebecca Finn and came to the United States.

For a short time he lived in Chicago and then moved to a farm near Cambridge where he remained for thirteen years. In 1851 he moved to Rock Island and engaged in the lumber business until 1858. Thereafter, he devoted himself to his lifetime hobby of entomology and was soon a recognized leader in the field. His first published entomological work appeared in 1860. In his lifetime he published 385 titles plus an additional 478 in collaboration with Charles V. Riley, another well-known entomologist. Walsh contributed regularly to the **Prairie Farmer, Valley Farmer,** and **Illinois Farmer,** was an editor of the **Practical Entomologist,** and was co-founder and editor of the **American Entolmogist** with Riley. His private collection numbered 30,000 insects. His insect studies impressed scientists and, perhaps more important, agriculturalists. He was one of the first to advocate that farmers use scientific methods to control insects.

His death on November 18, 1869 resulted from a railroad accident near Rock Island.

201

Bishop Hill, Illinois.

Illinois State Historical Library

Located: On US 34 at junction with spur leading to Bishop Hill.

BISHOP HILL

At Bishop Hill, two miles north of here, Eric Janson and Jonas Olson founded a colony of Swedish religious dissenters in 1846. Organized on communistic lines, the colony at one time had 1100 members and property worth a million dollars. Dissolution and the end of the venture came in 1862.

Located: Francis Park, N.E. of Kewanee.

WOODLAND PALACE

This was the home of Fred Francis, inventor and innovator, artist and poet. Born near Kewanee in 1856, he graduated from the Illinois Industrial University, Urbana, in 1878. While there, he was one of the designers and builders of the "Class of '78" clock, now in the North Tower of the Illini Union. In this home, which he built, he incorporated many innovations, including a water purification system and air conditioning. Francis died in 1926 and bequeathed this estate to the city of Kewanee, to be maintained as a city park and museum.

OFFICIAL STATE MAP: D-4
HENRY COUNTY

Located: rest area, east side of US 150, 3 miles south of Orion.

Illinois State Historical Library

Map of Illinois showing Military Tract.

MILITARY TRACT

Military land bounties were offered by the United States Government in the early national period to attract men into the Army or to reward soldiers for their services. Warrants were issued to the men for these bounties.

One of the three tracts created to meet the warrants given in the War of 1812 was located in the State of Illinois, in the triangle between the Mississippi and Illinois Rivers. The Northern Boundary, which extended ninety miles east from the Mississippi, is one mile north of here and ninety miles north of the base line of the Fourth Principal Meridian. The Illinois Tract, surveyed in 1815-1816, contained more than 5,000,000 acres, of which 3,500,000 were allocated to military bounties. Comprising 207 entire townships, each six miles square, and 61 fractional townships, the tract included fourteen present-day counties and parts of four others.

Soldiers of the War of 1812, who received 160 acres each, were required to locate their warrants by lottery. Most soldiers or their heirs decided, however, against moving great distances to take up their claims. Instead, they sold their warrants to speculators. One company alone acquired 900,000 acres.

Such large-scale land holdings aroused frontier hostility against absentee speculators. Squatters settled upon the lands, ignoring titles and rights. Many speculators were unable to realize a quick profit and, faced with ever-increasing taxation, lost their titles or sold their lands at a loss of money. Population growth, which was rapid in parts of the region from about 1823 to 1837, was retarded by conflicting land claims. Final adjustment of the claims was made only after years of litigations and much legislation.

203

ILLINOIS A HISTORY OF THE PRAIRIE STATE by Robert D. Howard, used by permission of William B. Erdman's Publishing Company

OFFICIAL STATE MAP: B-4
JO DAVIESS COUNTY

Located: On north side US 20 at Elizabeth, .5 mile east of town.

APPLE RIVER FORT

Here, during the Black Hawk War, was located Apple River Fort. On June 24, 1832, it was attacked by 200 warriors. Within were many women and children, but few men. Mrs. Elizabeth Armstrong rallied the women and inspired the defenders until relief arrived. Elizabeth is named in her honor.

THE DE SOTO HOUSE

Opened in April, 1855, the five-story, 240 room De Soto House was "the largest and most luxurious hotel in the West." Abraham Lincoln spoke from its balcony in 1856 and Stephen A. Douglas in 1858. Ulysses S. Grant maintained his 1868 presidential campaign headquarters here. By 1880 Galena's prosperity had faded and the hotel's two upper stories were removed.

Located: At De Soto House, Galena.

OFFICIAL STATE MAP A-4
JO DAVIESS COUNTY

Hotel De Soto, Galena, Illinois on US Highway 20.

Located: (1) Roadside park on the north side of US 20, 8½ miles east of Galena with "The Lead Mines". (2) Roadside park on the north side of US 20 at the junction of US 20 and Illinois 84 northwest of Galena.

OFFICIAL STATE MAP A-4
JO DAVIESS COUNTY

OFFICIAL STATE MAP A-4
JO DAVIESS COUNTY

Illinois State Historical Library

Looking Southwest from Seminary Hill across Franklin St., showing St. Mary's Catholic Church, Galena, Ill.

GALENA, ILLINOIS

Prior to 1820, Indians and occasional white traders occupied La Pointe, the name given to the present site of Galena. The settlement grew rapidly in 1823 and 1824 as each boat deposited new arrivals on the banks of the Fever (now Galena) River. The town was laid out in 1826, and the name changed to Galena (Latin for sulphide of lead). Terror reigned in the region during the Black Hawk War in 1832, but the suppression of the Indians cleared the way for unrestricted white settlement.

As supply center for the mines and shipping point for the growing river commerce, Galena became a thriving city when Chicago was still a swamp village. Galena's zenith arrived in the 1840's, and residents lavished money on elaborate houses, many of which still stand today. By the 1850's the surface lead deposits were depleted; the Galena River, once over 300 feet wide, began to gather silt; and the railroads started to take the river commerce.

Ulysses S. Grant arrived here in 1860 to work in his father's leather store. A year later this still obscure clerk marched off to the Civil War; in 1865, he returned in triumph to a gift mansion donated by his Galena neighbors. Grant was so prominent that he overshadowed the town's eight other Civil War generals.

In 1869, after his election as President of the United States, Grant appointed his Galena friends John A. Rawlins, secretary of war; Elihu B. Washburne, secretary of state; and Ely S. Parker, commissioner of Indian affairs.

THE LEAD MINES

The prehistoric glaciers which leveled most of Illinois left much of this Jo Daviess County area untouched. Thus, the lead and zinc ore deposits of the earth's bedrock remained on or near the surface. The Indians had a crude system of mining, and reports of their mines reached the French. About 1690 Nicholas Perrot visited the mines in this region, and in 1700 Pierre Charles Le Sueur took sample ore from the deposits along the Mississippi River. The great mining fields marked on early French maps, combined with glowing tales of upper Mississippi minerals, led John Law, a Scot promoter, to emphasize their possibilities in 1717. The French government became so involved in backing him that it bordered on bankruptcy when Law's "Mississippi Bubble" burst.

In 1822 Colonel Richard M. Johnson obtained the first lease from the federal government to mine lead around Galena, and he was given a military guard since the Fox Indians were still occupying the area. The United States Government expected to receive royalties on the lead produced but collection attempts failed, and in 1847 the lands were sold outright.

The lead mines around Galena reached their peak in 1845, when they produced about 83 per cent of the total United States output. Lead in the surface veins was finally exhausted in the 1850's, and without the necessary capital for intensive mining, lead production declined during the last half of the nineteenth century.

Located: Road side park on the north side of US 20, 8½ miles east of Galena with a Galena city market

OFFICIAL STATE MAP: A-4
JO DAVIESS COUNTY

Lead smelter near Galena -1841- from an old sketch.

Illinois State Historical Library

Located: Galena.

Illinois State Historical Library

Grant Statue, Grant Park, Galena.

GRANT'S HOME STATE MEMORIAL

When Ulysses S. Grant and his family arrived in Galena by steamboat from St. Louis in the spring of 1860, the city had already begun its economic decline. Galena experienced boom town prosperity from the lead mines in the 1820's and became a hustling river port and ambitious mercantile center in the 1840's.

Grant hoped to reverse his economic misfortunes by moving to northwest Illinois. Galena was the site of a leather goods store owned by his father, Jesse R. Grant, and operated by his brothers, Simpson and Orvil. In this store, Grant was nominally a clerk and "...travelled through the Northwest considerably during the winter of 1860-1. (They) had customers in all the little towns in south-west (sic) Wisconsin, south-east Minnesota and north-east Iowa." Until he left Galena in the spring of 1861 to serve in the Civil War, Grant and his family rented a modest, brick house on the west edge of the river.

On August 18, 1865, Galena greeted the return of its victorious general with a grand celebration. There was a jubilant procession, decorated arches, speeches and a holiday atmosphere. From a triumphal arch spanning Main Street, thirty-six young ladies dressed in white waved American flags and threw bouquets. During the ceremonies the citizens of Galena presented the furnished house on Bouthillier Street to the general.

General Grant and his family left for Washington, D.C. on September 12, 1865, where he continued his duties as commanding general of the Army. As most of his later trips, this visit was relatively short. The Grants returned to Galena in the fall of 1868 and remained throughout his successful campaign for the presidency.

During the next fifteen years the Grant family used their Galena home as a haven during the course of campaigns and long journeys. The general

Galena citizens welcome General Grant home from the war,
August 18, 1865.

STATE
MEMORIAL

enjoyed these brief periods renewing old friendships in Galena and the surrounding area.

After two terms in office, ex-President Grant and his family embarked, in May 1877, on a trip around the world. The Grants were warmly received by dignitaries in all of the countries they visited. Returning to San Francisco in September, 1879, the Grants made a triumphant journey to Galena. Their arrival "home" on November 5 prompted a large civic reception and celebration. Leaving in December, the general and his family returned to Galena only for short visits in 1880. As far as present research can tell, U.S. Grant left for New York City in September, 1880, and never stayed in his Galena house again, even though he and his wife visited Galena for one last time in May, 1883.

The brick house in the "Italianate Bracketed" style of the period was constructed as a residence for Alexander J. Jackson of Galena in 1859-1860. It was designed by William Dennison, "Engineer and Architect."

Elements of the style included in Grant's Home are: the well defined rectilinear blocks of the building, the projecting or overhanging eaves supported by brackets, the low pitched roof, the piazza or covered porch, and the balustraded balcony.

In 1940, Frederick Dent Grant, the eldest son, deeded the house to the City of Galena as a memorial to his father. The house was presented to the State of Illinois in 1932 and later incorporated into the Illinois Department of Conservation's Division of Parks and Memorials.

The original plans and specifications were available for guidance during restoration in 1955-57. At this time, the home was strengthened internally to handle the many visitors who tour it.

Grant Home, Galena, Ill.

OLD MARKET HOUSE STATE MEMORIAL

The Market House, built in 1845-1846 in the "Greek style," was the focal point of community life during Galena's prosperous decades. The Driftless Area, which had been bypassed by the glaciers, contained outcrops of lead sulfide and other minerals. It was these easily mined lead deposits that brought the first influx of American lead miners in the early 1820's. Lead mining was the economic mainstay of Galena until the 1850's.

The Fever (Galena) River provided an easy avenue for steamboat trade with St. Louis and other river cities. During the 1840's and 1950's as lead production declined, Galena thrived as a river port and commercial center. By 1860 railroads relocated regional trading centers, thus helping bring about the decline of the steamboat trade and Galena's economy.

In 1836 Congress authorized that the proceeds from the public sale of city lots be used for building wharves and public buildings in Galena. Two years later the city made plans to erect a market house with money collected from the sale of the city lots. Lack of funds delayed the city's plans until 1843.

Early in 1845 the city council passed an ordinance enabling the city to build a market house on Market Square and to raise funds by selling $2,500 worth of stock at $5.00 a share.

The city paid Slaymaker and Blish $100.00 for "plan and specification" of the Market House. The Superintendent of Ways and Bridges was authorized to advertise for sealed proposals for such a building "to be built of brick, and to be completed within six months from 'Plan No. 4,' available at Council Room." In February, 1845, the city council accepted Henry J. Stouffer's bid for the building of the Market House.

Historians have no absolute proof of who actually designed the Market House, but they do know that Henry Stouffer built several fine Galena

OFFICIAL STATE MAP:
JO DAVIESS COUNTY

Market House, Galena.

residences in the Greek Revival style. It must be noted that John L. Slaymaker and Thomas Blish were Galena Aldermen and members of the council's Market House Committee in 1845.

The City Council Chamber on the second floor was also used by local organizations for their meetings. Two city jail cells were built in the Market House basement in 1846.

The final cost of the Market House, will all additional work, was $3,104.16. The building was accepted by the city in January, 1846, and officially opened in July of that year.

The City Ordinances state that: ".....the entire market house, together with its appertenances, except such rooms as may be required for the use of the city council, city clerk, and market master, together with the market square, shall be rented by the market master....to individuals for the convenience of public marketing....The market of the city shall be open for the sale of all articles of victuals and provisions from the dawn of day until ten o'clock a.m., except on Saturday, when it shall be open from four p.m. until ten p.m., from the first day of April, until the first day of October, and from the dawn of day until twelve o'clock in the forenoon, during the remainder of the year."

The building ceased to be used as a market house in 1910. It was used by the city government and fire department until 1936. In 1947 the historic building, threatened with destruction, was donated by the City of Galena to the state of Illinois. During the mid-fifties the Market House was restored to its exterior appearance of 1846. Today it houses historical and architectural exhibits and is maintained by the Illinois Department of Conservation, Division of Parks and Memorials.

Located: Roadside park on U.S. 20, northwest of Galena, at junction of US 20 and Illinois 84 with a Galena city market.

THY WONDROUS STORY, ILLINOIS

The fertile prairies in Illinois attracted the attention of French trader Louis Jolliet and Father Jacques Marquette as they explored the Mississippi and Illinois Rivers in 1673. France claimed this region until 1763 when she surrendered it to Great Britain by the Treaty of Paris. During the American Revolution George Rogers Clark and his small army scored a bloodless victory when they captured Kaskaskia for the Commonwealth of Virginia, and Illinois became a county of Virginia. This area was ceded to the United States in 1784, and became in turn a part of the Northwest Territory and the Indiana and Illinois territories. On December 3, 1818, Illinois entered the Union as the twenty-first state.

Nathaniel Pope, congressional delegate from the Illinois Territory in 1818, persuaded Congress to set the northern border of the new state sixty miles about the previous line which had run from the southernmost tip of Lake Michigan to the Mississippi River. Thus, part of the lead mine region around Galena, the site of Chicago and the fourteen northern counties of the state became a part of Illinois.

Alarm spread across northwestern Illinois in 1832 when Black Hawk and a band of dissident Sauk and Fox Indians crossed the Mississippi River into Illinois. Stockades dotted the area until the defeat of the Indians cleared the way for increased white settlement.

SEE HISTORIC ILLINOIS

A war dance of the Sauk and Fox Indians whose defeat cleared the way for increased white settlement in Illinois.

Illinois State Historical Library

OFFICIAL STATE MAP B-8
KANE COUNTY

Located: Ill. 72, Sleepy Hollow

Illinois State Historical Library

Rev. William A. Sunday.

BILLY AND MA SUNDAY

Evangelist William "Billy" Sunday and his wife Helen "Ma" Sunday owned this farm, 1899-1913, and spent their summers here. Ma was born on the farm. Billy was born in Ames, Iowa, in 1862. He played the outfield for Chicago and other National League baseball clubs, 1883-1890. From 1896 until his death in 1935 he conducted religious revivals in cities and towns across the nation. His wife shared in his work. In May-June 1900 Billy led a month-long revival in West Dundee Park.

The famous Allan Pinkerton.

from PHOTOGRAPHIC HISTORY OF THE CIVIL WAR, vol. 8.

OFFICIAL STATE MAP: B-8
KANE COUNTY

Located: South 3rd & Main,
West Dundee

PINKERTON'S EARLY HOME

Allan Pinkerton, famous detective, had his home and cooperage on this lot, 1844-1850. Here he sheltered and employed slaves escaping to freedom. After helping to capture some counterfeiters, he became Deputy Sheriff of Kane County in 1848. In 1850 he founded his detective agency in Chicago. In February 1861 he was the bodyguard of President-Elect Abraham Lincoln on the train trip to Washington. Early in the Civil War he directed the spy service of the Union Army.

OFFICIAL STATE MAP: D-8
KENDALL COUNTY

Located: South side of US
34, 1¾ miles west of Plano

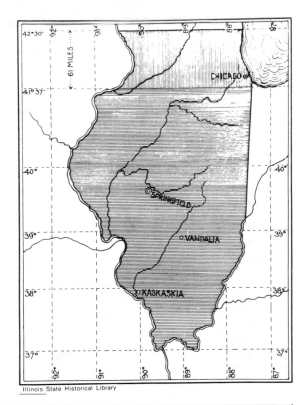

Illinois State Historical Library

THE NORTHERN BOUNDARY

The northern boundary of Illinois as prescribed in the Ordinance of 1787 was an east and west line from the southern tip of Lake Michigan at approximately 41 degrees, 37 minutes passing through this region to the Mississippi River. When Illinois applied for admission into the Union the bill included this boundary.

While the measure was still pending in the House, Nathaniel Pope, the Illinois delegate in Congress, felt the necessity of giving Illinois a firm footing on the lake thus committing her interest to northern commerce through the lakes to off-set the influence of the southern trade on the Mississippi and Ohio Rivers in case of future internal conflict. Pope felt that the territorial addition would, "afford additional security to the perpetuity of the Union, inasmuch as the State would thereby be connected with the states of Indiana, Ohio, Pennsylvania, and New York, through the Lakes." The amendment introduced by Pope making the boundary 42 degrees, 30 minutes, passed easily and the enabling act was approved on April 18, 1818.

Illinois gained approximately 61 miles of added territory including 14 counties covering 8500 square miles of fertile soil, lake and river ports, and such future prosperous cities as Chicago, Rockford, Freeport, and Galena. Politically, this additional northern territory decisively influenced Illinois in favor of national unity and against slavery during the Civil War period and was important in the nomination of Abraham Lincoln in 1860. Thus Pope's foresight had national repercussions as well as significance for Illinois.

THY WONDROUS STORY, ILLINOIS

The fertile prairies in Illinois attracted the attention of French trader Louis Jolliet and Father Jacques Marquette as they explored the Mississippi and Illinois Rivers in 1673. France claimed this region until 1763 when she surrendered it to Great Britain by the Treaty of Paris. During the American Revolution George Rogers Clark and his small army scored a bloodless victory when they captured Kaskaskia for the Commonwealth of Virginia, and Illinois became a county of Virginia. This area was ceded to the United States in 1784, and became in turn a part of the Northwest Territory and the Indiana and Illinois territories. On December 3, 1818, Illinois entered the Union as the twenty-first state.

US 41 leads directly into Chicago. About 1779 Jean Baptiste Point du Sable became the first permanent settler on the Chicago River. Twenty-four years later the United States established Fort Dearborn on the river. It was destroyed in 1812, later rebuilt, and garrisoned until 1836. Chicago was by then a thriving settlement, incorporated three years earlier and recognized as an ideal site for commercial development. The Illinois and Michigan Canal, completed in 1848, plus plank roads and railroads made the city the trade center of the Midwest.

Chicago citizens continually proved their vitality. In 1855, the city elevated its lowest streets eight feet to escape the effects of the marshes. On October 8, 1871, came the famous Chicago fire. Two days later plans were formulated for rebuilding the city and today Chicago stands as a world famous metropolis.

Jean Baptiste Point du Sable.

Located: West side US 41, 1 mile south of the Wisconsin state line.

OFFICIAL STATE MAP A-9
LAKE COUNTY

OFFICIAL STATE MAP A-9
LAKE COUNTY

Located: West side of US
45, 800 feet south of the
Wisconsin state line.

Illinois map.

THY WONDROUS STORY, ILLINOIS

The fertile prairies in Illinois attracted the attention of French trader Louis Jolliet and Father Jacques Marquette as they explored the Mississippi and Illinois Rivers in 1673. France claimed this region until 1763 when she surrendered it to Great Britain by the Treaty of Paris. During the American Revolution George Rogers Clark and his small army scored a bloodless victory when they captured Kaskaskia for the Commonwealth of Virginia, and Illinois became a county of Virginia. This area was ceded to the United States in 1784, and became in turn a part of the Northwest Territory and the Indiana and Illinois territories. On December 3, 1818, Illinois entered the Union as the twenty-first state.

Illinois acquired the fourteen northern counties, including the lead mine region around Galena and the site of Chicago, because of the foresight of Nathaniel Pope, congressional delegate from the Illinois Territory. His amendment to the statehood act moved the upper boundary from an east-west line through the tip of Lake Michigan to the present location. Within this region US 45 crosses the Des Plaines River which Jolliet and Marquette followed in 1673.

Between Kankakee and Effingham, US 45 parallels the Illinois Central, the first federal land grant railroad in the United States, and passes through the Lincoln country near Mattoon.

In southern Illinois this highway passes Fort Massac State Park, a site which the French fortified extensively in 1757. George Rogers Clark entered the Illinois country near it on his way to capture Kaskaskia.

217

Benjamin Lundy.

Located: At entrance to Starved Rock State Park with "Starved Rock" marker.

BENJAMIN LUNDY
1789-1839

Quaker newspaper editor of the abolitionist **Genius of Universal Emancipation** printed at Hennepin then Lowell, four miles south, November 8, 1838 to August 22, 1839. He had published it since 1821 in Ohio, Tennessee, Baltimore, Washington, D. C. and Philadelphia. Lundy is buried in Friends Cemetery near McNabb.

BUFFALO ROCK STATE PARK

Buffalo Rock State Park one mile south was the probable site of Fort Ottawa.

It was erected in 1760-61 by Captain Passerat la Chapelle and his French soldiers retreating from Canada to New Orleans to avoid surrender to the British.

Looking up the Illinois River towards Ottawa from Buffalo Rock State Park.
Illinois State Historical Library

OFFICIAL STATE MAP:
LASALLE COUNTY

Located: South side of U.S. 6, 4 miles East from Ill. 178

219

CANAL WAREHOUSE

This stone building was a warehouse on the Illinois and Michigan Canal. It was built by James Clark, a resident of Utica, one year after the canal was completed in 1848. Before the advent of the railroads the canal was the main commercial artery to Chicago. It helped establish Chicago as an important grain market and contributed greatly to the growth of that city and the northern part of the Illinois River Valley. Clark had also constructed five sections of the canal. He operated a general store in his warehouse, which shipped an average of 210,000 bushels of corn and 22,000 bushels of oats per year. It is the only surviving warehouse on canal frontage.

Located: I-80 LaSalle County Historical Society, Museum, Utica.

OFFICIAL STATE MAP D-7
LASALLE COUNTY

FIRST PERMANENT NORWEGIAN SETTLEMENT IN THE UNITED STATES

Here is commemorated the 100th anniversary of the first permanent Norwegian settlement in the United States by CLENG PEERSON and other pioneers from Norway. They and their descendants, who still live here, have contributed largely to the development of this section of Illinois.

Reshetched from Norlies History

Illinois State Historical Library

Cleng Peersons's Dugout.

OFFICIAL STATE MAP D-7
LASALLE COUNTY

Located: III 71, Norway

FORT JOHNSTON

On the eminence to the east stood Fort Johnston, headquarters of Gen. Henry Atkinson during part of the Black Hawk War. Here, May 27, 1832, Abraham Lincoln enlisted as a private in Elijah Iles' Company--his second enlistment of the war.

Located: At junction of Rts. 71 and 23, La Salle County

OFFICIAL STATE MAP D-7
LASALLE COUNTY

Illinois State Historical Library

Early forts such as Fort Johnston and Fort Wilbourne were built on bluffs overlooking the rivers to protect soldiers and settlers from surprise Indian attacks.

FORT WILBOURN

On the entrance to the southwest stood Fort Wilbourn, where the Third Army of Illinois Volunteers was mustered in for the service in the Black Hawk War.

Here on June 16, 1832 Abraham Lincoln enlisted as a private in Jacob M. Early's Company, his third enlistment of the war.

Located: U.S. 51, bridge, LaSalle

OFFICIAL STATE MAP: D-7
LASALLE COUNTY

221

Father Marquette discovering the Illinois Indians is shown passing Perrin's Ledge.

Located: On US 6, south side, 4 miles east of Ill. 178.

THE GREAT ILLINOIS VILLAGE

South of here the Great Village of the Illinois extended for three miles along the north side of the Illinois River. To this historic Indian town came La Salle, Tonti, Marquette, Allouez and other explorers and missionaries. Here, in September, 1680 the Iroquois attacked the Illinois, dispersed them and destroyed their village.

ILLINOIS AND MICHIGAN CANAL

This historic artery of travel was commenced in 1836 and finished in 1848. By carrying pioneers and their produce between Lake Michigan and the Illinois Valley, it figured largely in the development of northern Illinois. Superseded by the Deep Waterway after fifty years of use, it is now devoted to recreational purposes.

Located: Where State Rt. 23 crosses the canal at Ottawa

The Illinois and Michigan Canal.

INDIAN CREEK MASSACRE

On May 20, 1832, hostile Indians, mainly Potawatomi, massacred fifteen men, women and children of the Indian Creek settlement two miles to the west. Two girls, Rachel and Sylvia Hall, were carried into captivity and later ransomed. All had disregarded the warning of Shabbona, the white man's friend.

Located: On Rt. 23, west side, at junction with gravel road leading to Shabbona marker.

OFFICIAL STATE MAP: D-7
LASALLE COUNTY

LINCOLN-DOUGLAS DEBATE

On August 21, 1858, the first of the famous joint debates between Abraham Lincoln and Stephen A. Douglas was held in this park. Here 10,000 people heard the two contestants for the United States senatorship discuss the question of slavery in American politics.

OFFICIAL STATE MAP: D-7
LASALLE COUNTY

Illinois State Historical Library

Located: On west side of State Rt. 23 in Ottawa; in park just inside low stone well at inner edge of side walk and due east of boulder marking debate site.

An ambrotype of Abraham Lincoln made five days after Lincoln's debate with Stephen Douglas at Ottawa on August 21, 1858.

223

PERU-LA SALLE, ILLINOIS

The story of the twin cities of Peru and LaSalle is closely interwoven with the history of the Illinois River and the Illinois and Michigan Canal. In 1673 Jacques Marquette and Louis Jolliet passed through this area by way of the Illinois River enroute to Lake Michigan. The explorer Robert Cavelier, Sieur de LaSalle also came through here in 1680 and, in 1862-83, his lieutenant Henri de Tonti erected Fort St. Louis at Starved Rock to the east--now a state park.

Jolliet first noted the desirability of a canal connecting Lake Michigan to the Mississippi via the Illinois. In 1825 the Illinois and Michigan Canal Association was incorporated and in 1836 the Internal Improvements Act which included provision for a north-south railroad through Illinois was passed by the legislature. The fact that these important transportation facilities were to converge in this area encouraged further settlement. Peru, organized in 1834, was incorporated in 1838. Although the advantage at first rested with Peru, activity eventually shifted to LaSalle since the boat basin of the canal and the railroad routes were finally located there. While settlers were here as early as 1830, LaSalle was not incorporated until 1852.

Construction on the canal was begun in 1836 and completed in 1848. It extended from the Chicago River to Peru-LaSalle and was an important trade link for thirty years. Two railroads, completed to LaSalle in the 1850's, eventually replaced the canal in importance, and the emphasis in the twin cities gradually shifted from transportation to mining and industry.

OFFICIAL STATE MAP: D-7
LASALLE COUNTY

Located: (1) On the west side of US Business 51, south of LaSalle. (2) U.S. 6, south of St. Bede Academy.

Illinois State Historical Library

Robert Cavalier, Sieru de LaSalle.

Starved Rock, the site of Fort St. Louis.

Illinois State Historical Library

Located: At entrance to Starved Rock State Park, with "Benjamin Lundy" marked.

OFFICIAL STATE MAP: LASALLE COUNTY

STARVED ROCK

This was the site of Fort St. Louis, erected by the French traders LaSalle and Tonti in 1682. For the following ten years Fort St. Louis was the center of French influence in Illinois. According to tradition, a band of Illinois Indians was besieged here in 1769 by northern tribes seeking to avenge the murder of the Ottawa Chief Pontiac. Stranded on the rock and unable to secure provisions, the Illinois band died of starvation. The site became known as "Starved Rock" from that legend.

Located: US 52 North bank
of Rock River, Dixon

Illinois State Historical Library
The Lincoln monument in Dixon, Illinois.

ABRAHAM LINCOLN

Was stationed here during the Black Hawk War in 1832 as captain of volunteers. On April 21, 1832, he enlisted at Richland Creek, Sangamon County, and was elected captain. He was mustered into state service at Beardstown on April 22 and into United States service at the mouth of Rock River May 3. At the mouth of Fox River on May 27, he was mustered out and on the same day re-enlisted as a private in Captain Elijah Iles' Company.

At the expiration of this enlistment, he re-enlisted on June 16, at Fort Wilbourn in Captain Jacob M. Early's Company, and was finally mustered out of service on July 10, 1832, at White Water River, Wisconsin.

226

DIXON, ILLINOIS

In 1828 Joseph Ogee established a ferry across the Rock River where Dixon now stands. In 1830, John Dixon, postmaster, moved to the site with his family to operate the ferry which had prospered because of its location on the trail between the Galena lead mines and Peoria. The name of the small settlement was soon changed from Ogee's Ferry to Dixon's Ferry. John Dixon--"Father Dixon" to the settlers and "Nachusa" (white haired) to the Indians--was a community leader until his death on July 6, 1876. Dixon became the county seat in 1839 and is today a thriving community.

At the beginning of the Black Hawk War in 1832 a small fort was built on the north bank of the river. Among the men of future prominence who served here were Abraham Lincoln and Zachary Taylor, U. S. Presidents; Winfield Scott, presidential nominee and famous soldier; Robert Anderson; Albert Sidney Johnston and Joseph E. Johnston, Civil War generals; William S. Hamilton, son of Alexander; Jefferson Davis, President of the Confederacy; and John Reynolds, Illinois governor. The statue, "Lincoln, the Soldier," by Leonard Grunelle stands on the site of Fort Dixon.

In 1837 Alexander Charters obtained a tract of land three miles north of Dixon's Ferry. He named his estate Hazelwood and entertained such notables as William Cullen Bryant, Stephen A. Douglas, Abraham Lincoln, and General Philip Kearney. Charles Walgreen who lived in Dixon as a youth and later founded the Walgreen drugstores, purchased Hazelwood in 1929.

Located: In a rest area on the south side of Illinois 2 or US Alt. 30, three and a half miles west of Dixon.

OFFICIAL STATE MAP: C-6
LEE COUNTY

The Fort Dixon Memorial depicts John Dixon founder of the city of Dixon.

Illinois State Historical Library

227

OFFICIAL STATE MAP C-6
LEE COUNTY

26

Located: Dixon, Illinois

LINCOLN IN THE BLACK HAWK WAR

On May 12, 1832 Captain Abraham Lincoln's Company of Illinois Volunteers camped one mile west. Lincoln re-enlisted in two other companies and was frequently in Dixon. Discharged from service near Fort Atkinson, Wisconsin, on July 10, Lincoln passed through Dixon enroute to New Salem.

MORMONS IN AMBOY

The reorganized Church of Jesus Christ of Latter Day Saints was established in 1852 in southern Wisconsin. On April 6, 1860, Joseph Smith III, son of the Mormon founder, was ordained President-Prophet of the reorganized church. The ceremony was held at Goldman's Hall, which stood on this site at Amboy. A Morman congregation had been organized here about 1840. Smith headed the reorganized church until his death in 1914. Church headquarters was founded at Plano, Illinois in 1866, moved to Lamoni, Iowa, in 1881, and to Independence, Missouri, in 1921.

Joseph Smith III.

Illinois State Historical Library

52

OFFICIAL STATE MAP: C-6
LEE COUNTY

Located: East Avenue near Main, Amboy.

228

Located: West side of Illinois 14, 1200 feet south of the Wisconsin line near Harvard

OFFICIAL STATE MAP: A-8
MCHENRY COUNTY

THY WONDROUS STORY, ILLINOIS

SEE HISTORIC ILLINOIS

The fertile prairies in Illinois attracted the attention of French trader Louis Jolliet and Father Jacques Marquette as they explored the Mississippi and Illinois Rivers in 1673. France claimed this region until 1763 when she surrendered it to Great Britain by the Treaty of Paris. During the American Revolution George Rogers Clark and his small army scored a bloodless victory when they captured Kaskaskia for the Commonwealth of Virginia, and Illinois became a county of Virginia. This area was ceded to the United States in 1784, and became in turn a part of the Northwest Territory and the Indiana and Illinois territories. On December 3, 1818, Illinois entered the Union as the twenty-first state.

The bill under which Illinois applied for entry into the Union described her northern boundary as a line running west from the southern tip of Lake Michigan as prescribed in the Ordinance of 1787.

Nathaniel Pope, congressional delegate from the Territory of Illinois, succeeded in establishing the present boundary while the bill was still pending. Pope argued before Congress that the boundary 61 miles farther north would "afford additional security to the perpetuity of the Union, inasmuch as the State would thereby be connected with the States of Indiana, Ohio, Pennsylvania, and New York, through the Lakes." This tie with northern interests would offset the southern influence of the Mississippi River trade. This proved important during the Civil War period. The altered boundary also gave Illinois the lead mine region around Galena and the fourteen northern counties.

229

OFFICIAL STATE MAP: A-8
MCHENRY COUNTY

Located: West side of US 12, ¾ miles south of Wisconsin line near Richmond.

THY WONDROUS STORY, ILLINOIS

SEE HISTORIC ILLINOIS

The fertile prairies in Illinois attracted the attention of French trader Louis Jolliet and Father Jacques Marquette as they explored the Mississippi and Illinois Rivers in 1673. France claimed this region until 1763 when she surrendered it to Great Britain by the Treaty of Paris. During the American Revolution George Rogers Clark and his small army scored a bloodless victory when they captured Kaskaskia for the Commonwealth of Virginia, and Illinois became a county of Virginia. This area was ceded to the United States in 1784, and became in turn a part of the Northwest Territory and the Indiana and Illinois territories. On December 3, 1818, Illinois entered the Union as the twenty-first state.

Illinois acquired the fourteen northern counties, including the site of Chicago, because of the foresight of Nathaniel Pope, congressional delegate from the Illinois Territory. His amendment to the statehood act moved the upper boundary from an east-west line through the tip of Lake Michigan to the present location.

Before the first settlers came, this territory was a hunting ground for the Potawatomi Indians who traded their furs with hunters coming up the Fox River. Lake Zurich was founded by Seth Paine, abolitionist and free-thinker, who settled there in 1836 and built his "Stable of Humanity." This building included a meeting hall, school, and store and provided lodging for unfortunate families. At one time Paine considered all civil law, including marriage and taxes, a form of slavery. In later life he went to Chicago where he continued his philanthropy.

Located: Ill 26, Oregon Blacktop east of Polo.

OFFICIAL STATE MAP: C-5
OGLE COUNTY

BOLES TRAIL

In 1825 Oliver W. Kellogg blazed a trail from Peoria to Galena which passed east of this site. On a spring day in the following year John Boles marked a shorter route near this point. The news of the Boles Trail spread and it became a heavily traveled route for the next three years.

Located: Ill. 26, Milledge-ville Road, west of Polo.

OFFICIAL STATE MAP: C-5
OGLE COUNTY

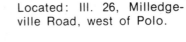

BUFFALO GROVE

The Indians called this area Nanusha (buffalo). The first settlers arrived here in 1829 and six years later a village, St. Marion, was laid out. About 1840 the name was changed to Buffalo Grove and the village prospered until 1855 when the railroad steamed through Polo. Naturalist John Burroughs taught here in 1856-1857.

Located: Grand Detour, John Deere Blacksmith Shop recreation

Illinois State Historical Library

Following his own design, John Deere makes his first self-scouring steel plow in 1842 in this Illinois sesquicentennial painting.

THE FIRST STEEL PLOW

In his blacksmith shop located on this lot, John Deere made the first successful steel plow in 1837. In contrast to previous models Deere's plow, with its steel share and carefully shaped mold board, turned the sticky black earth polishing itself clean and thus helped open the vast rich prairies to agricultural development.

Located: US 52 south of Polo

THE GALENA ROAD

In the early 1830's pioneer traffic moving north from Peoria crowded primitive trails and forced a direct route to Galena. In 1833 Levi Warner's state survey marked the "Balena Road." It cut through this schoolyard. Private Abraham Lincoln passed this site June 13, 1832 in Captain Elijah Ile's Black Hawk War Company.

Located: Southeast side of
Illinois 2. .4 mile north of
Grand Detour.

GRAND DETOUR, ILLINOIS

Early French traders who traveled the Rock River named the large bend southwest of this point, Grand Detour. Winnebago and Potawatomi villages in the area made it a prominent location for fur trading posts, and during the 1820's the United States Government granted licenses to traders at "Grand Detour on Rocky River."

Permanent settlement at Grand Detour began after Leonard Andrus traveled up the Rock River in 1834 in search of a town site. Impressed by the natural beauty of the region and the power and transportation potential of the river, Andrus claimed the land and in 1836 laid out a village.

A year later John Deere, a Vermont blacksmith, settled in Grand Detour. While working in his shop, Deere heard farmers lament that the rich Illinois soil stuck to the wooden and iron plows they had brought from the East. Deere tackled the problem and shaped a steel plow out of a discarded saw blade from the Andrus sawmill. The soil slid smoothly off the highly polished steel surface, and as the demand for his plows increased, Deere began production using steel imported from England and later from Pennsylvania. High freight costs forced him to seek better transportation facilities, and in 1847 he moved from Grand Detour to Moline, Illinois, on the Mississippi River, where he began manufacturing plows in quantity.

Since the Rock River was never developed for navigation and the railroads bypassed the community, Grand Detour retains much of its nineteenth-century atmosphere.

The Andrus "Plouch" Manufactory was where John Deere made his first steel plow.   Illinois State Historical Library

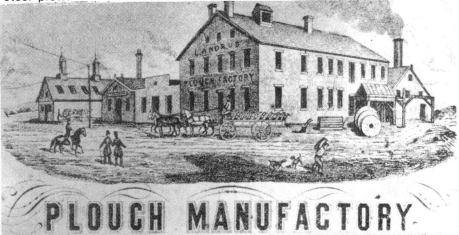

PLOUCH MANUFACTORY.

Located: 1½ miles west of Polo on Eagle Point Road

INDIAN AMBUSH

Early in the Black Hawk War Indians concealed near this spot in Buffalo Grove, May 19, 1832, killed William Durley, a member of a six man detail carrying despatches (sic) from Colonel James M. Strode at Galena to General Henry Atkinson at Dixon's Ferry. Durley's body now rests beneath this memorial.

Located: 123 N. Franklin, Polo

LINCOLN IN POLO

Abraham Lincoln was a guest in this house, August 15-17, 1856. His host was Zenas Aplington, founder of Polo. On Saturday, August 16, John D. Campbell and James W. Carpenter, who were law partners in Polo, joined Lincoln and Aplington in a drive by carriage to Oregon, Ogle County seat. There Lincoln and "Long John" Wentworth, six-term congressman and later mayor of Chicago, were among several speakers at a political rally for John C. Fremont, first Republican presidential candidate.

THE REGULATORS AND THE BANDITTI

In the 1830's and 1840's an organized criminal gang known as the Banditti of the Prairie was active on the midwestern frontier. In 1841 six members were arrested and held for trial in Oregon, Illinois. On March 21, the day before the trial, the new Oregon Courthouse was burned. In retaliation, a group led by W. S. Wellington organized the Regulators and ordered several suspected Banditti to emigrate or be whipped. Some left but those remaining forced Wellington to resign as Regulator leader. He was replaced by John Campbell.

John Driscoll, a Banditti leader, and his four sons (Pierce, William, David, and Taylor) made a career of horse stealing and murder. When the Regulators gave the Driscolls 20 days to leave Illinois, the Banditti decided to kill Campbell and Phineas Chaney, another Regulator leader. Chaney escaped but on June 27, 1841, Campbell was killed by David and Taylor while John, William, and Pierce waited nearby. John was caught and jailed at Oregon. The Regulators apprehended William and Pierce and forcibly took John from jail. The three were "tried" in Washington Grove on June 29 by a jury of 111 Regulators. Pierce was released but the other two were found guilty. John was shot by 56 men and William by 55. Although Banditti activity continued for several years, it was no longer centered in Ogle County.

The Regulator judge and jury (112 men) were tried for the vigilante murder of the Driscolls and were acquitted.

OFFICIAL STATE MAP: C-6
OGLE COUNTY

Located: Rest area, east side of Ill. 2, about 6 miles north of Oregon.

235

Illinois State Historical Library
Mount Morris College

Located: College Grounds, Wesley A v e n u e, Mount Morris

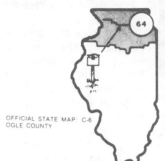

OFFICIAL STATE MAP: C-6
OGLE COUNTY

MOUNT MORRIS COLLEGE

Rock River Seminary, the first institution of higher education in northern Illinois, was established by the Methodist Church in 1839. Because of financial difficulties it was forced to close in 1879. The Church of the Brethren then purchased the campus and established Mount Morris Seminary and Collegiate Institute. In 1884 the name was changed to Mount Morris College. This building, "Old Sandstone," was reconstructed in 1912, after the original "Old Sandstone," built in the 1850's, was partially destroyed by fire. Mount Morris College closed in 1932.

STILLMAN'S DEFEAT

Here, on May 14, 1832, the first engagement of the Black Hawk War took place, when 275 Illinois militiamen under Maj. Isaiah Stillman were put to flight by Black Hawk and his warriors. So thoroughly demoralized were the volunteers that a new army had to be called into the field.

OFFICIAL STATE MAP: B-6
OGLE COUNTY

Located: On Rt. 72 at eastern edge of Stillman Valley

236

THOMAS FORD

Thomas Ford, eighth governor of Illinois, was born in Pennsylvania in 1800 and came to Illinois in 1805, with the aid of his half-brother, George Forquer. He received some advanced education and studied law. He practiced law at Waterloo and, in partnership with Forquer, at Edwardsville. From 1829 to 1835 he served as prosecuting attorney for all of the state west and north of the Illinois River.

On January 14, 1835, the State Legislature elected Ford judge of the Sixth Judicial Circuit, which then included all counties in the northern quarter of the state. Soon after that date and until he was elected governor, Ford made his residence here in Ogle County. He became judge of the Chicao Municipal Court in 1837. In 1839 he was elected judge of the Ninth Circuit, comprised of nine counties between the Rock and the Fox and the Illinois Rivers.

In 1841 a Democratic-controlled State Legislature enlarged the Supreme Court to nine men, who doubled as circuit judges. Ford was named to the court and reassigned to the Ninth Circuit. He sat on the bench in Oregon during the last days of a band of outlaws called the Banditti of the Prairie.

Ford was elected governor as a Democrat in August 1842. When he took office in December, he faced a critical state debt and the Mormon troubles. He refused to repudiate the debt and secured adoption of a plan to liquidate it. Both before and after the murder of Joseph Smith, the Mormon prophet, Ford called out the militia to preserve order between Mormons and their foes. At the end of his term Ford resumed the practice of law in Peoria, where he died in 1850. His **History of Illinois** was published posthumously.

OFFICIAL STATE MAP: C-6
OGLE COUNTY

Located: Courthouse. Ill. 2
& 64. Oregon

Illinois State Historical Library

Thomas Ford, eighth governor of Illinois.

BLACK HAWK WAR CAMPSITE

In 1832 when Black Hawk and his Sauk and Fox followers returned to Illinois, 1500 mounted volunteers advanced along the banks of the Rock River to capture them. 505 men under Colonel Zachary Taylor followed in supply boats and late at night on May 12, 1832 camped in this area.

Black Hawk.

Illinois State Historical Library

OFFICIAL STATE MAP: D-3
ROCK ISLAND COUNTY

Located: Rock River Bridge at Hillsdale.

CAMPBELL'S ISLAND

At Campbell's Island, approximately one mile northwest of this point, Indians led by Black Hawk attacked a force of US regulars and rangers under Lieutenant John Campbell on July 19, 1814. The Americans were defeated with a loss of sixteen killed.

Located: In triangle formed by State Rt. 80 and road leading to Campbell's Island. West side Rt. 80 at north edge of East Moline.

OFFICIAL STATE MAP: D-3
ROCK ISLAND COUNTY

FORT ARMSTRONG

Fort Armstrong was built in 1816-1817. Its riverside was protected by limestone bluffs and its other sides were formed in part by the rear walls of barracks and storehouses. Blockhouses, like the replica, stood at three corners. The pyramid of cannon balls to the southwest marks the site of the northeastern blockhouse. The fort was garrisoned by United States troops until May 4, 1836. It served as headquarters for the Sauk and Fox Indian agent from 1836 to 1838 and as a military depot from 1840 to 1845. It was destroyed by fire in 1855.

OFFICIAL STATE MAP:
ROCK ISLAND COUNTY

Located: Rock Island Arsenal

A view of Fort Armstrong, Rock Island, Mississippi River. Illinois State Historical Library

239

Located: On west side US 67
at intersection of Tarvia road
running west to Andalusia
south of Milan.

LINCOLN AND THE BLACK HAWK WAR

On May 8, 1832, while encamped approximately one mile west of this point, Abraham Lincoln was mustered into the military service of the United States. A few days earlier he had been elected captain of a militia company from Sangamon County.

ROCK ISLAND AND ROCK ISLAND ARSENAL

Rock Island, surrounded by the waters of the Mississippi, played a significant part in the opening of the West. The Indians in the area early recognized the stratetic advantage of the island and held ceremonial gatherings here. Nearby, at Campbell and Credit Islands, were fought the westernmost campaigns of the War of 1812. Fort Armstrong, at the lower end of Rock Island, was garrisoned from 1816 to 1836, and the Black Hawk War ended here in 1832. Among the troops that served in this vicinity were future Presidents Zachary Taylor and Abraham Lincoln. The island was the home of Indian trader George Davenport.

The support of a terminal of the first bridge to cross the Mississippi River rested on the island. Two weeks after the bridge was opened in 1856, the steamer **Effie Afton** rammed a pier, setting it afire, and the drawspan was destroyed. Abraham Lincoln represented the railroad interests in the lawsuit that followed.

A prison for captured confederate soldiers was maintained on the island from 1863 to 1865. Rock Island Arsenal was established here in 1862 as one of three in the Midwest. It has served the nation through all wars and conflicts since 1898. Today, besides being the location of the arsenal, the Island is the site of headquarters, U.S. Army Weapons Command, plus the arsenal's John M. Browning Museum and several other federal agencies. It is also the site of one of the world's time capsules.

Located: Arsenal Memorial Park. Rock Island

OFFICIAL STATE MAP.
ROCK ISLAND COUNTY

Rock Island Arsenal.

Illinois State Historical Library

241

Site of the Battle of Bad Axe, the final defeat of Black Hawk on August 2, 1832.

OFFICIAL STATE MAP: D-3
ROCK ISLAND COUNTY

Located: US 6, ½ mile west of the junction of US 6 and Illinois 84 near Rock Island.

THY WONDROUS STORY, ILLINOIS

SEE HISTORIC ILLINOIS

The fertile prairies in Illinois attracted the attention of French trader Louis Jolliet and Father Jacques Marquette as they explored the Mississippi and Illinois Rivers in 1673. France claimed this region until 1763 when she surrendered it to Great Britain by the Treaty of Paris. During the American Revolution George Rogers Clark and his small army scored a bloodless victory when they captured Kaskaskia for the Commonwealth of Virginia, and Illinois became a county of Virginia. This area was ceded to the United States in 1784, and became in turn a part of the Northwest Territory and the Indiana and Illinois territories. On December 3, 1818, Illinois entered the Union as the twenty-first state.

The Sauk and Fox Indians settled throughout this region early in the eighteenth century. The largest Sauk Village, Saukenuk, located several miles to the west on the point between the Rock and Mississippi Rivers, contained about one hundred lodges and over one thousand warriors at the height of its strength.

The United States obtained this area through a treaty in St. Louis on November 3, 1804. Black Hawk, a leading warrior, did not consider the treaty binding. Although the Sauk nation left Saukenuk in 1829, Black Hawk and his band returned twice in the next two years. He retired west of the Mississippi in 1831 after militiamen burned Saukenuk but returned the final time the following year resulting in the Black Hawk War. His final defeat was on August 2, 1832, in the Battle of Bad Axe.

THY WONDROUS STORY, ILLINOIS

The fertile prairies in Illinois attracted the attention of French trader Louis Jolliet and Father Jacques Marquette as they explored the Mississippi and Illinois Rivers in 1673. France claimed this region until 1763 when she surrendered it to Great Britain by the Treaty of Paris. During the American Revolution George Rogers Clark and his small army scored a bloodless victory when they captured Kaskaskia for the Commonwealth of Virginia, and Illinois became a county of Virginia. This area was ceded to the United States in 1784, and became in turn a part of the Northwest Territory and the Indiana and Illinois territories. On December 3, 1818, Illinois entered the Union as the twenty-first state.
Illinois entered the Union as the twenty-first state.

A railroad bridge which was located between the Government Bridge and US 67 on the Mississippi at Rock Island figured prominently in one of the most important of Abraham Lincoln's law cases. Despite strenuous objections by the river interests, the bridge was constructed there in 1856. The bridge, built to aid railroad expansion beyond the Mississippi, was to leave river traffic unobstructed. However, on May 5, 1856, the steamboat **Effie Afton** rammed it and burned. The disaster renewed the controversy between the river interests and the railroads, and the steamboat owner sued the bridge company.

The company retained Lincoln and others. Thoroughly familiarizing himself with the case, Lincoln handled the defense and obtained a hung jury--in reality a victory for the railroads. The case remained unsettled for years, during which time the westward expansion of the railroads continued uninterrupted.

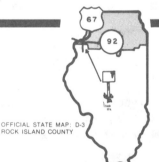

Located: East side of US 67, 2 miles south of the junction of US 67 and Illinois 92 in Milan

OFFICIAL STATE MAP: D-3
ROCK ISLAND COUNTY

Rock Island, Illinois and the Mississippi River.
Illinois State Historical Library

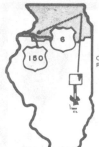

OFFICIAL STATE MAP: D-3
ROCK ISLAND COUNTY

Located: East side of US 150. ½ mile south of the junction of US 150 and US 6 near Rock Island.

THY WONDROUS STORY, ILLINOIS

SEE HISTORIC ILLINOIS

The fertile prairies in Illinois attracted the attention of French trader Louis Jolliet and Father Marquette as they explored the Mississippi and Illinois Rivers in 1673. France claimed this region until 1763 when she surrendered it to Great Britain by the Treaty of Paris. During the American Revolution George Rogers Clark and his small army scored a bloodless victory when they captured Kaskaskia for the Commonwealth of Virginia, and Illinois became a county of Virginia. This area was ceded to the United States in 1784, and became in turn a part of the Northwest Territory and the Indiana and Illinois territories. On December 3, 1818, Illinois entered the Union as the twenty-first state.

In 1854 Secretary of War Jefferson Davis recommended that an arsenal be established in the Midwest. Twenty-five years earlier Congress had reserved Rock Island in the Mississippi for military use. From 1816 until 1836 Fort Armstrong had been located there.

The coming of the Civil War emphasized the importance of a midwestern arsenal. Congress authorized a small arsenal on the island on July 11, 1862 as one of three arsenals in the Midwest. Then in 1865 it was decided to make Rock Island a major arsenal. While the main section was not completed until 1893, several smaller arsenals were combined at Rock Island from 1871 to 1891. In every crisis from the Spanish-American War through the Korean conflict, the arsenal has expanded and it is today one of the finest in the world.

Illinois State Historical Library

The Rock Island Arsenal.

CEDARVILLE

Birthplace of Jane Addams 1860-1935. Humanitarian, feminist, social worker, reformer, educator, author, publicist. Founder of Hull House, Pioneer Settlement Center, Chicago, 1889. President, Women's International League for Peace and Freedom. Nobel Peace Price, 1931.

OFFICIAL STATE MAP: B-5
STEPHENSON COUNTY

Located: North edge of Cedarville on west side of Ill. 26.

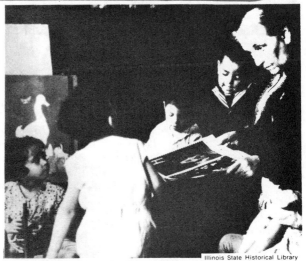

Illinois State Historical Library

Jane Addams, Nobel Peace Prize winner of 1931.

Located: On south side US 20 at gravel road 4.9 miles east of Rt. 78, or ¼ mile west of Kent Road.

OFFICIAL STATE MAP: B-5
STEPHENSON COUNTY

KELLOGG'S GROVE

At Kellogg's Grove, four miles south of here, two engagements were fought during the Black Hawk War. On June 16, 1832, Capt. A.W. Snyder's Company defeated a band of Indians; but on June 25, Indians led by Black Hawk defeated Maj. John Dement's battalion of volunteers.

LINCOLN-DOUGLAS DEBATE

On August 27, 1858, Abraham Lincoln and Stephen A. Douglas, on a platform erected near State and Douglas Streets, met in the second of their seven joint debates. Douglas' answer to Lincoln's "Freeport Question" helped to win the senatorial race, but was fatal to his presidential prospects two years later.

OFFICIAL STATE MAP B-5
STEPHENSON COUNTY

Located: (1) One marker on fence line on S. side US 20 at west city limits. Freeport; (2) One marker at intersection Ill. 26 & Mini Airport Road. East side Ill. 26 just north of city limits, Freeport.

OFFICIAL STATE MAP B-5
STEPHENSON COUNTY

Stephen A. Douglas

OFFICIAL STATE MAP: C-4
WHITESIDE COUNTY

Located: Post Office, Fulton

Illinois State Historical Library

Dement House, Fulton.

DEMENT HOUSE

Dement House, an imposing stone hotel, was built on this lot in 1855. The owner suffered financial setbacks, partly due to the relocation of the depot in Fulton, and the hotel was sold to satisfy judgements in 1858. At various times thereafter the building was used to house two military academies, a veterans' college, a coeducational college, and a tire factory. It was razed in 1934.

OFFICIAL STATE MAP: C-4
WHITESIDE COUNTY

Located: 16th St. & 8th Ave.,
Northeast section of Fulton

FULTON'S FIRST HOME

John Baker, Fulton's first permanent settler, arrived in 1835 and built his three-room log cabin and outbuildings nearby. He lived in amity with the Indians and kept a rude hostelry. Later Fulton's first doctors, Daniel and Lucinda Reed, made the cabin their home, practiced medicine and also entertained travelers.

Illinois State Historical Library

Hennepin Canal, lock tender closing hand operated gate.

OFFICIAL STATE MAP: C-4
WHITESIDE COUNTY

Located: Rock River, Rock Falls

ILLINOIS AND MISSISSIPPI CANAL

Construction on the "Hennepin Canal," as it was commonly known, began in 1892 and was completed in 1907 at a cost of more than seven million dollars. The main canal extended 75 miles from the Illinois River near Hennepin to the Rock River near its juncture with the Mississippi. A feeder canal from the Rock River at Rock Falls joined the main canal 29 miles to the south near Mineral. Utilization of the Hennepin Canal never reached expected proportions because of rapid technological advances in other modes of transportation, and in 1951 it was closed to traffic.

Robert L. Wilson, member of the "Long Nine"
of the Illinois legislature during the 1830's.

Located: 607 East Third,
Sterling

OFFICIAL STATE MAP C-5
WHITESIDE COUNTY

LINCOLN IN STERLING

On July 18, 1856, Abraham Lincoln spent the night in this house as the guest of William Manahan. Lincoln had been invited by Robert Lange Wilson to address a John C. Fremont rally in Sterling. Wilson was a member of the famous Long Nine of the Ilinois Legislature during the 1830's.

THE MARKET PLACE

Early Fulton communal activity centered around this trigon. The ferry, powered successively by man, horse, and steam, landed at its north end. Stores, hotels, warehouses and saloons faced all three sides. Later the sawmills rented it to store huge piles of lumber. It became a city park in 1958.

OFFICIAL STATE MAP: C-4
WHITESIDE COUNTY

Located: At the foot of eighth avenue in River Front Park, Fulton.

Fulton, Illinois, 1880.

249

Henry M. Kennedy.

Illinois State Historical Library

Located: 707 Fourth, Fulton

MODERN WOODMEN

This house was the head office of the Modern Woodmen of America, a fraternal life insurance society, when that organization first became an Illinois co rporation in 1884. The house was the home of Dr. Henry M. Kennedy, head clerk of the fraternal society from 1884 to 1888. The society was founded in 1883 by Joseph C. Root of Lyons, Iowa. Between 1886 and 1897 the office occupied three other sites in Fulton before being moved to Rock Island, where it is presently located.

PROPHETSTOWN

Prophetstown occupies the site of the village of the Winnebago Prophet, which the Illinois volunteers destroyed on May 10, 1832, in the first act of hostility in the Black Hawk War.

Located: On Rts. 78-226 in landscaped triangle at north end of village.

OFFICIAL STATE MAP:
WHITESIDE COUNTY

Located: North side of US
30. 6 miles east of junction
of US 30 and Illinois 84 near
Fulton.

George B. Armstrong.

THY WONDROUS STORY, ILLINOIS

The fertile prairies in Illinois attracted the attention of French trader Louis Jolliet and Father Jacques Marquette as they explored the Mississippi and Illinois Rivers in 1673. France claimed this region until 1763 when she surrendered it to Great Britain by the Treaty of Paris. During the American Revolution George Rogers Clark and his small army scored a bloodless victory when they captured Kaskaskia for the Commonwealth of Virginia, and Illinois became a county of Virginia. This area was ceded to the United States in 1784, and became in turn a part of the Northwest Territory and the Indiana and Illinois territories. On December 3, 1818, Illinois entered the Union as the twenty-first state.

Illinois acquired the fourteen northern counties, including the lead mine region around Galena and the site of Chicago, because of the foresight of Nathaniel Pope, congressional delegate from the Illinois Territory. His amendment to the statehood act moved the upper boundary from an east-west line through the tip of Lake Michigan to the present location.

In 1864 the Chicago and North Western Railway tracks betweenchicago and this site carried the first railway post office in the United States. Under the old system the mail pouches had been delayed in one or more distributing post offices until the agents could sort it. Assistant Postmaster George B. Armstrong of Chicago devised a plan for a crew of clerks to sort and re-sack the mail as the train sped along the tracks.

The Illinois and Michigan Canal, April 9, 1865.

Located: On US 6 at Channahon. North side of road and east of canal in approach to State Park.

ILLINOIS AND MICHIGAN CANAL

This historic artery of travel was begun in 1836 and finished in 1848. By carrying pioneers and their produce between Lake Michigan and the Illinois Valley, it figured largely in the development of northern Illinois. Superseded by the Deep Waterway after fifty years of use, it is now devoted to recreational purposes.

ILLINOIS AND MICHIGAN CANAL OFFICE

In 1837 the town of Lockport was laid out by the Illinois and Michigan Canal commissioners and a residence office was built. The first floor of the permnent structure was completed in 1837, and became headquarters for construction and administration of the waterway. The canal, which extended ninety-six miles from the south branch of the Chicago River near Lake Michigan to the Illinois River at Peru, was in operation from 1848 to 1914. This building, now owned by the Will County Historical Society, houses the Illinois and Michigan Canal Museum.

Located: Canal Office, 801 S. State, Lockport.

Located: Industrial road
west of Larken Avenue,
South of Joliet

MICHIGAN & ILLINOIS CANAL

1331

Joliet Mound

JOLIET MOUND

This is the site of Mont Joliet, a natural eminence named for the explorer Louis Joliet. It was 1350 feet long and 225 feet wide, with a flat top and steep escarpment, rising 140 feet above the Des Plaines River bed, or 60 feet above the bank. First shown on a 1674 map, the mound served for almost 175 years as a landmark for measuring distances on the river route from Chicago to the Mississippi. Completion of the Illinis and Michigan Canal in 1848 obviated the need for this information. The mound has since been leveled by quarrying.

Located: 503 Main, Plain-
field

PLAINFIELD HOUSE

This was the site of the Arnold Tavern, first government franchised post office in present day Will County (1834-1845). The present building was the home of Dr. E.C. Wight, one of the first physicians in northern Illinois (1836). and a post-house which accommodated Chicago-Ottawa stage line passengers (1836-1886).

Camp Grant shown during World War I.

Located: On Rt. 2 at bridge, south of Rockford, leading to Camp Grant

CAMP GRANT

Camp Grant, one-half mile to the east, was established in 1917. Here was trained the 86th, or Black Hawk Division, of the National Army. Camp Grant was abandoned as a post in 1921.

ROCKFORD COLLEGE

This plot of land is the original site of Rockford College, chartered in 1847 as Rockford Female Seminary. Students were enrolled in 1851. Bachelor's degrees were first conferred in 1882. One of five recipients that year was Jane Addams, who was to gain fame as a social reformer. Ten years later the school's present name was adopted. When the college became cocducational in 1955, it began an expansion program that led to relocation on the new campus in 1964.

Located: Division & South Second, Rockford

Rockford College.

Located: 6 miles northeast
of Rockford on US 51N-I 11.
173NE. 3½ miles southwest
at junction III. 2 and F.A. 179

OFFICIAL STATE MAP B-7
WINNEBAGO COUNTY

OFFICIAL STATE MAP B-7
WINNEBAGO COUNTY

ROCKFORD, ILLINOIS

On August 24, 1834, Thatcher Blake, Germanicus Kent, and two others settled on the west side of the Rock River ford and built a sawmill on Kent Creek. The following year Daniel Haight settled on the river's east bank. Kentville and Haightville combined to form Rockford in 1835.

Following the Polish Rebellion of 1830-31, exiles sought refuge in this country and in 1834 Congress granted them their choice of 36 sections of land in Illinois or Michigan. In 1836 Count Louis Chlopicki chose sections in this area, ignoring the occupants. However, these sections were not adjacent as the act specified they should be, and the "Polish Claim" was voided, thus ending a serious threat to the claims of the earlier settlers of Rockford and vicinity.

Rockford became the home of John H. Manny, a leading manufacturer of agricultural implements, in 1853. His reaper was quite successful, but inventor Cyrus McCormick sued Manny for infringements of patent rights. The defense lawyers, including Abraham Lincoln and Edwin M. Stanton--later in Lincoln's cabinet--won the case in 1856.

The Forest City Nine became nationally known in 1867 by defeating the top ranking Washington Nationals. In 1869-70 they defeated practically every important professional and amateur team in the country. Alumni of this famous baseball team included A.G. Spalding, Roscoe Barnes, and Adrian C. Anson.

Miss Julia C. Lathrop of Rockford was the first woman to head a U.S. government agency. President William H. Taft appointed her Chief of the Children's Bureau in Washington in 1912. She retained this position under President Woodrow Wilson.

Illinois State Historical Library

Julia C. Lathrop of Rockford who was the first woman to head a United States government agency. She was appointed chief of the Children's Bureau by President William H. Taft in 1912.

Galena, Illinois

OFFICIAL STATE MAP: A-7
WINNEBAGO COUNTY

Located: US 51 at the east
edge of South Beloit

THY WONDROUS STORY, ILLINOIS

The fertile prairies in Illinois attracted the attention of French trader Louis Jolliet and Father Jacques Marquette as they explored the Mississippi and Illinois Rivers in 1673. France claimed this region until 1763 when she surrendered it to Great Britain by the Treaty of Paris. During the American Revolution George Rogers Clark and his small army scored a bloodless victory when they captured Kaskaskia for the Commonwealth of Virginia, and Illinois became a county of Virginia. This area was ceded to the United States in 1784, and became in turn a part of the Northwest Territory and the Indiana and Illinois territories. On December 3, 1818, Illinois entered the Union as the twenty-first state.

Illinois acquired the fourteen northern counties, including the lead mine region around Galena and the site of Chicago, because of the foresight of Nathaniel Pope, congressional delegate from the Illinois Territory. His amendment to the statehood act moved the upper boundary from an east-west line through the tip of Lake Michigan to the present location.

In 1832 a band of Sauk and fox Indians under Black Hawk entered Illinois near Rock Island and headed up the Rock River with the army in pursuit. Both groups passed through this area on their way to the final encounter at the Battle of Bad Axe.

The Third Principal Meridian, which U.S. 51 roughly parallels, was a basic line in surveying the Northwest Territory to establish definite land claims.

CHICAGO SITES

The history of Chicago began with the coming of Father Jacques Marquette, of France, priest of the Society of Jesus, who, on his mission to the Illinois Indians arrived at the Chicago river Dec. 4, 1674.

Chicago has erected many monuments, tablets and statues to commemorate its past. Listed here are just a few of the better known Chicago landmarks.

Fort Dearborn: South end of Rush Street Bridge. One of the military posts established by Thomas Jefferson to protect the new frontier. Built by Captain John Whistler in 1803. Destroyed by Indians, August 16, 1812--the day after the Massacre.
Located: Tablet in London Guarantee and Accident Building, 360 N. Michigan Ave., Southwest corner at Wacker Drive.

South Water Street: This was Chicago's main business street in 1834, connecting the village with Fort Dearborn. Years before this also was the site of a trading post with the Indians.
Located: Now Wacker Drive between State and Clark streets.

Old Water Tower: This Water Tower, completed in 1869, marks the establishment of Chicago's second water works and stands as a memorial of the Fire of 1871. It is the only complete structure in the path of fire that now stands.
Located: At Chicago and Michigan avenue.

Mrs. O'Leary's Home: On this site stood home and barn of Mrs. O'Leary where the Chicago Fire of 1871 started. Although there are many versions of the story of its origin the real cause of the fire has never been determined.
Located: 558 DeKoren Street. Tablet erected by CHS.

Kennison, David: A granite boulder marks the grave of David Kennison - the last survivor of the Boston Tea Party. Died Chicago at age 115 yrs.
Located: Boulder in Lincoln Park, near the intersection of Wisconsin and Clark streets.

The Wigwam: Temporary wooden building erected 1860, for the Republican National Convention. Here Abraham Lincoln was nominated for the first time for the presidency.
Located: Site of Franklin McVeagh Building - Southeast corner of Lake and Wacker Drive. Tablet on building.

Ogden Home: The home of Mahlon D. Ogden, was the only house in the path of the Chicago Fire which was not burned. It is now the site of the Newberry Library.
Located: Tablet on building, 60 West Walton Place.

Two new types of historical markers will be erected by the Illinois State Historical Society in 1976. Five special markers, commemorating the American Revolution in Illinois, will have distinguishing red, white, and blue trim.

The second new type, a large aluminum plaque, will eventually replace the large plywood historical markers presently in use. The first large aluminum marker will be erected at the point where the Third Principal Meridian intersects its Base Line. The Meridian is the subject of the marker.

For additional information or updated lists of Illinois State Historical Markers contact:

Mr. Ozzie Reynolds
Historical Markers Supervisor
Illinois State Historical Society
Old State Capitol 62706

COUNTY INDEX

Illustration Index

259

Illustration Index

Illustration Index

General Index

General Index

General Index

General Index

General Index

General Index

General Index

General Index

General Index

General Index

General Index

All spelling, punctuation and capitalization done in accordance with Webster's Unabridged Dictionary. Any exceptions recommended by the Illinois State Historical Society.